HOW TO DIFFERENTIATE LEARNING

In A Nutshell

series

HOW TO DIFFERENTIATE LEARNING

Curriculum, Instruction, Assessment

In A Nutshell
collection

Robin J. Fogarty • Brian M. Pete

CORWIN
A SAGE Company

For information:

Corwin
A SAGE Company
2455 Teller Road
Thousand Oaks,
    California 91320
(800) 233-9936
Fax: (800) 417-2466
www.corwinpress.com

SAGE Ltd.
1 Oliver's Yard
55 City Road
London EC1Y 1SP
United Kingdom

SAGE India Pvt. Ltd.
B 1/I 1 Mohan Cooperative
    Industrial Area
Mathura Road,
    New Delhi 110 044
India

SAGE Asia-Pacific Pte. Ltd.
33 Pekin Street #02-01
Far East Square
Singapore 048763

Printed in the United States of America

A catalog record of this book is available from the Library of Congress.

ISBN: 978-0-9763-4261-8

This book is printed on acid-free paper.

        10   11   12   13   10   9   8   7   6   5   4   3   2

Contents

Introduction

While seasoned staff know that there really is nothing new in education, from time to time, a compelling concept is revisited which such gusto that it almost takes on a life of its own. This is the case with the concept of differentiated learning. It is not a new idea, by any means, as evidenced by such terms as personalised instruction, individualised learning contract and individual education plan (IEP). Yet, the concept of differentiating learning has captured the attention of educators across the many continents.

According to Carol Ann Tomlinson (1998), 'Three principles from brain research – emotional safety, appropriate challenge and self-constructed meaning – suggest that a one-size-fits-all approach to classroom teaching is ineffective for most students and harmful to some'. Differentiating learning is not about teaching louder and slower. It's about a robust instructional repertoire. It's about having an assortment of teaching tools and techniques to meet the diverse needs of students. It's about different strokes for different folks, and about different entry points and end points to learning!

Based on Tomlinson's conceptual model, differentiation is about change, challenge and choice in today's classroom: Change the content! Change the process! Change the product! It's about the opportunity to learn through the many ways of knowing and expressing what one knows. Differentiation is

Differentiation is about change, challenge and choice.

about standards-based instruction and brain-based learning. It's about high quality teaching that targets how students learn best.

This is the second book on differentiation from the *In a Nutshell* series. The first book is titled *Differentiating Learning: Different Strokes for Different Folks*, by Robin Fogarty.

■□■□■

Chapter 1: Definition and rationale

This chapter is about defining the concept of differentiation in both formal and informal ways. In addition to a comprehensive look at what differentiation means, this chapter also focuses on the rationale that supports it. Teachers are given a look at how students are identified as individuals and as flexible skill groups for differentiated instruction. In brief, the essence of this chapter is to introduce the concept of differentiation and the rationale for it, as well as to place the strategy within the context of a standards-based curriculum.

The chapter addresses the following questions:

What is differentiation?

How does differentiation relate to standards-based learning?

What is meant by a 'teaching repertoire' for differentiation?

What is the rationale for differentiated learning?

How does data support differentiation?

What is differentiation?

Differentiation refers to the concept of meeting the individual needs of each learner, of customising instruction to help students learn. Carol Ann Tomlinson (1999) defines differentiated instruction by suggesting that differentiation is changing something: the content, the process or the product. (The informal definition, in a more folksy manner, is 'different strokes for different folks'.) It's about matching the teacher's teaching to the student's learning. It's about determining appropriate instruction by student likes, student interests and student profiles.

Synonyms for differentiated include: personalised, individualised, customised, tailored, 'tweaked', modified, adjusted, adapted, accommodated, stylised, manipulated, and fine-tuned. The best, most clarifying synonyms are personalised instruction or individualised instruction; the most helpful idea is about 'tweaking' a basic lesson for the developing learner or for the advanced learner.

Personalised, individualised, customised, tailored, 'tweaked,' modified, adjusted, adapted, accommodated, stylised, manipulated and fine-tuned.

Analogies that clarify differentiation include: Differentiation is like a movie, because both leave the participant with different views. Differentiation is like a balloon, because both take you to new heights. Differentiation is like a mobile phone because both can be highly personalised.

How does differentiation relate to standards-based learning?

The two concepts of standards – standards for all students and differentiation for each student – sound like diametrically opposed and conflicting ideas. How can teachers teach the same standard curriculum to all and at the same time teach differently to each, according to individual needs, talents and abilities? Yet, the message is actually quite consistent: the standards are 'the what' and the differentiation is 'the how' (Tomlinson, 1999). The two concepts, in effect, complement each

The standards are 'the what' and the differentiation is 'the how'.

other and speak to teachers about their 'best practices' in the classroom.

Standards of learning speak to the curriculum content that is delineated for the learners. Subject matter content outlined in the standards sets expectations for exactly what students should know and be able to do. Typically, the *content standards* include principles, facts and data, concepts and skills, while *process standards* include attitudes, dispositions, habits of mind and life skills such as problem-solving, teamwork and communication. These standards are nested into the lesson that targets content standards.

Differentiated learning speaks to the methods by which learning occurs, within the framework of the standards, to the diversity of the learners and to their myriad approaches to learning. It's about a repertoire of teaching strategies. There must be many ways for students to learn and to demonstrate their learning and, at the same time, the standards of learning, or the goals of the curriculum, must remain constant.

When these two concepts work together, students become the focus of schooling. They are exposed to a standard curriculum that sets high expectations for each and every student's achievement and, at the same time, students are allowed to learn content in personally relevant ways. Both the teaching and learning processes are fully honoured: The standards honour the accepted curriculum that teachers are required to teach and are held accountable for; and differentiated learning honours the full range of diverse learners found in most classrooms.

What is meant by a teaching repertoire for differentiation?

Teachers must have a robust instructional repertoire if they are to reach the needs, talents and abilities of various students; they need a repertoire of strategies to structure the teaching/learning process individually for each student. In other words, teachers must have a broad spectrum of instructional, curricular and assessment methodologies.

Teachers must have a rich and versatile set of teaching tools and techniques to structure the learning processes for the diversity of children in their classrooms. Teachers in today's schools need multiple ways to tap into the many kinds of minds. As one senior teacher once said, 'Teaching differently doesn't mean teaching the same thing louder and slower. It does not mean special education classes, gifted education, learning resource rooms or pull-out and push-in programs. It's not about labelling, sorting or disenfranchising any student in any way. In fact, it's the antithesis of these things. It's about honouring the uniqueness of each student.'

'It's about honouring the uniqueness of each student.'

How do teachers differentiate instruction?

To differentiate instruction, teachers must change something substantive – the content, the process or the product (Tomlinson, 1999) – and they must effect these changes within the context of challenge and choice. Differentiation is about welcoming each and every learner, in celebration of the differences of each one. It's about a robust instructional repertoire that teachers tap into as they try to reach and teach each student.

Differentiation is about change, challenge and choice in today's classroom: Change the content! Change the process! Change the product! Change the pacing! Change the environment! (Fogarty, 2001) Change something! It's about the opportunity for teachers to use varied methods of instruction to meet the diverse needs of students in that classroom.

Differentiation is about standards-based learning and high quality teaching. It's about accepting each and every learner that comes our way, and expecting the best from each and every one of them. Quality teaching means challenging students, requiring rigour in their learning, leaving nothing to chance, making no excuses and teaching with a results-oriented approach.

> **Differentiation is about standards-based learning and high quality teaching.**

What is the rationale for differentiated learning?

There are a number of reasons that educators around the world are interested in this complex process called differentiation. Reasons include: diverse multicultural demographics; myriad English language learners (ELL); local initiatives and state and federal mandates for inclusive classrooms; the rising mobility of society as a whole; and last, but not least, the emergent science of the brain and learning.

Multicultural

Perhaps a primary reason that differentiated instruction has become a global interest is that, in many cases, the school itself has taken on

> **... differentiated instruction has become a global interest ...**

the features of a global village. Most schools have widely diverse demographics, with a plethora of cultures residing within the walls of one small building, or one centralised school area. To meet the diverse needs of these learners and, at the same time, to honour their cultural norms, requires a differentiated approach to learning in the K–12 classroom.

Multiple languages

Paralleling the cultural mosaic is the mixture of multiple languages represented by this varied and rapidly growing international population. The number of English language learners (ELL) is exploding in all schools – predominantly those in our large urban centres. With this influx of countless languages, the need for differentiation screams out to the leaders and policy-makers of our schools.

Least restrictive environment

Couched in a philosophy of choosing the concept of inclusive classrooms – and/or with the official mandate for inclusion as the 'least restrictive environment' for each and every learner – classrooms are now fully integrated. Children with physical and mental challenges of all kinds, as well as students with a far-reaching range of learning disorders are part and parcel of regular classroom dynamics. Differentiation is the only effective way to address these many and varied needs.

Mobility of families

Unlike any time in history, the ability for families to move from one part of the country to another is unprecedented. Corporate moves, immigrants, climate-oriented relocations and even minor moves within the school catchment zones are all reasons that school populations are more transitory than ever before. With these constantly changing demographics, differentiated instruction is front and centre on the instructional agenda.

Brain science

The most compelling rationale for differentiation comes with the study of the brain and learning. Brain science is currently an explosive field, with the advent of brain imaging techniques that are discovering the story of the brain and how it learns. The well-accepted fact that each brain is unique sets the stage for differentiating learning in our classrooms. Each brain has a different set of wiring, because each person has different DNA and different environmental influences. Differentiated classrooms recognise this and tailor learning opportunities accordingly.

> **The most compelling rationale for differentiation comes with the study of the brain and learning.**

In summation, differentiation is one response to the many kinds of minds we find in one classroom, one school or one district. In fact, differentiation is the only reasoned response to the multitude of differences we find in our academic world.

> **Differentiation is the only reasoned response to the multitude of differences we find in our academic world.**

How does data support differentiation?

State tests, or textbook tests, provide comprehensive information about what students know and are able to do. These tests are often aligned to the standards and provide valuable feedback on the state of things for each learner. This data is often sorted by skills and available for flexible skill groupings in the classroom.

Classroom assessment provides the daily 'read' on how things are going for each student. Through work samples, quizzes, interactions and various and sundry other methods, teachers have their finger on the pulse of the learners. Self-assessment data are necessary kinds of data if students are to become self-regulating learners. They need to be reflective about their own strengths and weaknesses in order to be able to adjust and compensate. Observational data from the teacher are invaluable in monitoring and adjusting flexible skill groups. The teacher uses the observed data to make quick and relevant decisions for particular students.

Data is often sorted by skills and available for flexible skill groupings.

Data on student interests provide viable information for student groupings that automatically differentiate by interest and motivation. When students have a choice, they are more invested in the tasks; they take ownership. Student learning profiles also provide a wealth of information to differentiated learning.

Local assessments provide on-going feedback on student progress. The data are points along the way, rather than summative data at the end of the process when it's too late to alter and adjust anything. Summative data are like performing an autopsy. It's over. It's too late. Formative data are like reading a heart monitor. The numbers give you instant, relative feedback to act upon at various intervention points along the way.

Activity 1: A story that tells the story

Read the following story to a colleague. When you are done, pose the question at the end of the story, then talk about it.

Does the teacher lower the prize or do they give the student a chair?

A story that tells the story of differentiation

Imagine three mysterious intriguing prizes hanging on a wall. They are all hanging from a level bar, all at the same height, which represents the idea of a standard. Now, three students reach for the prizes. One student, the tallest of the three, reaches the prize with little or no effort at all. The second student reaches the prize, but only after stretching as high as they possibly can standing on their tip-toes. Finally, the third student is not able to reach the prize, even when standing on their tiptoes and stretching as much as they can. In terms of differentiating learning, the question is this: Does the teacher lower the prize or do they give the student a chair? That's the essence of the concept of differentiation, in a nutshell!

Activity 2: Read and review

Read one journal article/book by Carol Ann Tomlinson, University of Virginia. Visit the ASCD website for a full listing at www.ascd.org.

What do you think?

Review the following agree/disagree statements and respond to each. After you have finished, discuss your answers with a partner.

1. Differentiating learning is just an instructional strategy renamed.

2. Uniformity is NOT a synonym for differentiation.

3. Differentiation is a brain-based strategy for the classroom.

4. The rationale for differentiation includes: One size fits all.

5. A standards-based curriculum and differentiation for individuals are complex concepts to marry.

6. A robust teaching repertoire means that teachers must have a toolbox of instructional strategies.

7. Classroom assessment data are more important than state test data.

8. Differentiation is often mandated.

9. The rationale for differentiating instruction is convincing.

10. Differentiation is an instructional strategy that is both brain-based and standards-based.

Inside the classroom and beyond

To extend your understanding of differentiation, discuss your ideas with two colleagues: one who is a beginning teacher and one who is quite experienced. Compare their responses to what you believe you understand about differentiation at this point.

Chapter 2: Differentiated learning

This chapter introduces the elements of the conceptual model for differentiating learning as discussed by Tomlinson (1999). It delineates the ways teachers change the lessons to adapt to the various needs of the learners they teach. In addition, this chapter compares and contrasts traditional classrooms to classrooms in which differentiation is implemented.

This chapter addresses the following questions:

What are the elements of differentiation?

What does it mean to differentiate instruction by changing the content?

What does it mean to differentiate instruction by changing the process?

What does it mean to differentiate instruction by changing the product?

How do teachers prepare for differentiating instruction?

How do differentiated classrooms compare to traditional classrooms?

What are the elements of differentiation?

Three elements seem pertinent to the concept of differentiation: change, challenge and choice. First is the element of *changing* something to make the learning more accessible to all learners. Second is the element of *challenging* all learners at their level of understanding. Third is the element of allowing students to have some real *choice* in the teaching/learning process. Something substantive must change: the content, the process or the product (Tomlinson, 1999).

Change

To change the content, teachers might change the instructional input by offering historical information through a non-fictional text, a novel of historical fiction or even a biography of a significant player of the era. The standards of learning haven't changed, but the vehicle for presenting content is varied to suit different learners.

> **To change the content, teachers might change the instructional input ...**

To change the process, teachers might change the students' working arrangements by partnering students together to prepare an assignment or having individuals attack an assignment alone. In each case, the students are responsible for the learning, but there are varied techniques to assist the learner in that process.

To change the product, teachers might change the requirements for an assignment and encourage one group to enact a dramatic role-play of an event, another group to give a puppet show depicting similar information, a third group to prepare a scholarly paper and yet another group to present a musical rendition of the information under study. This way, students can all address the same set of content standards to create a product, but they are allowed, and encouraged, to use entry points that work well for them.

Different content vehicles, different processing strategies and different culminating products should be available for students to demonstrate their learning. That's what differentiated learning means: changing something of essence in the teaching and/or in the learning.

Challenge

Challenge engages the brain (Caine and Caine 1991; Diamond 1998; Fogarty 1997; Jensen 1998; Sousa 1995; Sylwester 1995). More specifically, challenge alerts the attention system in the brain. It gets the brain to pay attention to what is going on in the immediate environment. Because short-term memory precedes the processes of putting things into long-term memory and storing information for later retrieval, the importance of challenge in the classroom is quite significant. These are the elements that hook the emotions and alert the attention system in the human brain. Memory and learning involve novelty, relevance, meaning, dissonance and engagement

When something is new, the brain pays attention to that novelty. For example, when the teacher brings in a new text for the students early in the year, students actually are drawn to look through the book. It is novel and their curiosity is piqued. This concept easily becomes a way to differentiate.

When something is new, the brain pays attention to that novelty.

If the brain hears something that is of relevance, it pays attention to what's coming next. It is on alert and looks for a relevant connection. For an illustration of how important relevance is in tapping into the emotional brain, think about how quickly some students pay attention when the teacher says, 'It's going to be on the test.' This is extremely relevant information to students eager to get good

Think about how quickly students pay attention when the teacher says, 'It's going to be on the test.'

marks. Or, think about how eager kids are to learn imperial measurement as they construct a model to scale. Of course what is relevant to one student may not be as relevant to another, so the teacher facilitates differentiation with this idea of individual student relevance.

The brain seeks meaning (Caine & Caine 1991). It constantly processes information, looking for critical connections and ways to make meaning. If the brain can make sense of incoming input, it has a way to connect it, to pattern it and to chunk it with existing ideas already in long-term memory.

An example of making meaning is when the teacher connects the human body system to other 'systems' such as the economic system or the political system. Suddenly, the brain has a pattern that is reinforced and makes sense for the concept of systems. Differentiation is part and parcel of individual students constructing their own meaning. That construction of meaning is unique to each.

The brain also pays attention when something does not make sense or is a surprise. Two simple illustrations make the point here. First, when a person responds to a joke, the person's brain, which was focused on one stream of thought, suddenly taps an entirely different pattern or connection. This causes a cognitive jolt. Second, when someone says a contradictory statement such as, 'The brain is like a sieve!' the mind pays attention and says, 'What? The brain is like a sponge! Isn't it?' Notice how there is some emotional impact to hearing the opposite of what one believes. Using dissonance is a strategy for differentiation.

The brain also pays attention when something does not make sense or is a surprise.

■ □ ■ □ ■

These are the elements that teachers must use to hook into the short–term memory system of learners. But, the real emotional hook, in terms of rigour and challenges that stimulate the neural networks, occurs when and only when there is time to engage in the challenge (Diamond 1998). Engagement, as seminally defined by Csikszentmihalyi (1990), describes a state of mind he called FLOW. In FLOW, the learner is so deeply engaged in the task that time passes with little awareness by the learner who is immersed in thought. What engages one student may not engage another. Yet, engagement is the goal in differentiating instruction.

Choice

'Different strokes for different folks' means choice. It means opportunity for students to select the 'what' or the 'how' of the learning situation. It means choices about which of three books they will read, or which of the twenty events they will choose to write an essay on. It means choices about how they will demonstrate their learning, based on three of the eight multiple intelligences (Gardner 1999): verbal–linguistic, visual–spatial, bodily–kinesthetic, logical–mathematical, musical–rhythmic, interpersonal, intrapersonal and naturalist. The structure is determined by the teacher, but with choice built in.

The structure is determined by the teacher, but with choice built in.

Choice doesn't mean complete freedom for students to decide everything about the teaching/learning process. Choice means freedom to choose within a given structure. It has definite parameters that align with the expectations of the learning environment. It is generally accepted that students learn more when they

Choice means freedom to choose within a given structure.

■ □ ■ □ ■

feel they have some choice about what, when and how to learn; when they have had some voice in the process; and when they feel ownership in the decision about their own learning.

What does it mean to differentiate instruction by changing the content?

To change something in the teaching/learning process with challenge and choice, there are three aspects of content that afford opportunity for real differentiation. These three areas include: changing the *complexity* of the content, changing the *resources* used to convey the content and changing the learning *environment* of the content.

Complexity

Teachers can differentiate instruction by changing the complexity. They can strategically use three tiers of learning for students to change the complexity of the content and provide various levels of challenge and appropriate student choices. The most basic level of complexity is the *concrete* level in which students use objects to learn. The next tier of content complexity is the *symbolic* level in which the content is represented in pictures or illustrations. The third tier of content complexity is the *abstract* level, in which words and ideas are used to convey a learning experience. Skillful teachers, that is teachers with rich repertoires, know how to orchestrate all three tiers to challenge students.

An example of designing learning opportunities for the three tiers – concrete, symbolic and abstract – is illustrated in a lesson on rocks. At the concrete level, the students work with the rocks to engage in a hands-on investigation. At the symbolic level, students view a video about rock formations and then draw scientific diagrams depicting the direction of the various instances and methods. At the abstract level, textbook readings might be complemented by an informative lecture from an expert. Students might discuss the sophisticated concepts of rock formations, earthquakes, volcanic eruptions and glacial movement.

To change content complexity, the teacher may set up three stations, each of which uses one of the three tiers for students to experience the learning in a way that suits them. Or the teacher may actually use all three tiers in a series of lessons, calling for students to join if they choose to learn in a certain way or if they choose to revisit an idea in another way. Or the teacher may simply scaffold all three tiers for the whole class when complex concepts are introduced.

Resources

To change the content by differentiating resources is another option for the teacher in the diverse classrooms of today. Different publishers take different approaches for learning: they provide textbooks, contemporary journals and magazines and/or fictional accounts of the event or topic. The skillful teacher uses an array of these resources, matching learners and methods, to plan new materials for learning.

This model of changing resources is used frequently with novel studies. Using this strategy, the teacher may list myriad resources that deal with the topic. Each resource

Each resource addresses the same idea, but it offers a different entry point into the learning.

addresses the same idea, but it offers a different entry point into the learning.

In another example, some students may prefer to study about stem-cell research by reading the textbook; others may enjoy learning through a biographical rendition of the issue; still others may want to see a film or search the Internet for recent news articles; and some students may want to analyse political cartoons for meaning and relevance to this sensitive issue. Within this diversity of resources, students find the entry points that work for them. They eventually explore other methods demonstrated by fellow students that they may learn to like as well.

Environment

In essence, by changing the learning environment the content inherently changes too.

To change the learning environment is yet another method of differentiating the content. Learning environments include the classroom environment, of course, but also the school, the neighborhood, the community and even the virtual environment of technology. In essence, by changing the learning environment the content inherently changes too.

One brief example illustrates changing content by changing the environment. Imagine a child learning about quilting by reading about it in a school classroom. Then, imagine the same child learning about quilting in the living room of their grandmother's house. Finally, imagine that child learning about quilting by visiting a museum that presents a live quilting demonstration. In each instance, the child is learning similar content, but in very different environments that dictate a particular perspective on that content.

A more 'schoolish' kind of content involving changing the environment is the study of software applications. While studying *Excel*, for example, students are invited to work with the content in several different learning environments: they may choose to work in the classroom developing their own spreadsheets; students may decide to work in the resource centre, doing research about how to apply spreadsheets to business; or they may elect to work with a community business partner and investigate how the software is applied in a real company.

Changing the environment changes what the learner experiences about the topic or theme under study. Just by virtue of being in a different environment the student learns about the subject-matter content quite differently. Although the idea of changing the learning environment seems like a lot of work for teachers, after they start thinking about the learning environment many unsuspected opportunities afford themselves. In the beginning, it becomes a matter of valuing the concept of differentiated learning. After using the strategy of differentiating the learning environment it becomes a matter of course in the planning process.

What does it mean to differentiate instruction by changing the process?

The lesson elements represent the science of teaching, whereas the changes in how the elements are used represent the art of teaching. Creative teachers craft lessons in ways that are unique and inviting to students. They present *direct instruction* of concepts, skills and attitudes in lesson designs that create moments of surprise, of intrigue, and of inquiry. They change how they involve students in authentic and real ways, prior to, during and after the learning. To change the process by incorporating various *cooperative learning* structures is one way to differentiate learning. Inquiry is yet another process to use.

Direct instruction

Changing the method of direct instruction is something that most teachers already do naturally. Madeline Hunter (1971) identified seven elements of lesson design: anticipatory set, learning objectives, input, modelling, guided practice, feedback and independent practice. To change the direct instruction model, the elements don't really change, but the execution of the elements changes – the order of the elements shifts, hence, the process is changed. These teachers change the *anticipatory set*, the *input* and the *practice*.

Seven elements of lesson design: anticipatory set, learning objectives, input, modelling, guided practice, feedback and independent practice.

To change the *anticipatory set*, teachers must find creative ways to get the focused attention of students. They must find unique methods to get students to anticipate what is coming next and to hook them into the learning with some enticement. For instance, they might use a cartoon, a riddle, a challenging problem, a game, a compelling story, a surprise guest, a walk, an interview, a video piece or a poem as effective methods to develop an anticipatory set.

To change the *input*, teachers must use a repertoire of methodologies to get the information across to students. They must design with skill and ease and bring originality to the learning situation. Good craftsman use lectures and mini-lectures, of course, but they also use investigations, problem-solving, case studies, video and film segments, computer software, games, the Internet, debates, guest speakers and excursions to help students achieve deep understanding.

To change the *practice*, teachers must know how to shift the skill-and-drill kinds of guided practice to compelling contests, games and relays. They must structure practices that are focused and brief and others that are intensely involving. Ideally they would design independent practice as homework assignments that require thought and care, as well as in-school assignments that help students to try things out on their own.

Cooperative learning

Cooperative structures range from two students working together in duos, as partners, in think/pair/share arrangements; to trios with two partners working and one observing; to small groups of four or five students with appropriate roles and responsibilities.

TTYPA ..., or 'Turn to your partner and ...' (Fogarty, 1990), is an easy, informal partner interaction that is used to punctuate a long talk or film. Duos make a great team for preparing a presentation of some sort or working in a debate mode. Think/pair/share is another partner strategy that requires 'two heads together'. First, the individuals think on their own, then they interact as a pair and talk about their ideas and, finally, they present a 'shared' opinion, having reached some agreement.

> **TTYPA ..., or 'Turn to your partner and ...' (Fogarty, 1990), is an easy, informal partner interaction.**

The use of trios is another cooperative structure that allows for a partner interaction with a built-in observer. Or the threesome might work together as a small group with various roles and responsibilities required to complete the task. They might have a recorder, a reporter and a leader.

Cooperative groups may be used in a more formal setting, with three to five students arranged in a heterogeneous grouping. The roles and responsibilities vary depending on the complexity of the tasks. But, with small groups, there is a need to incorporate explicit social skill instruction (Johnson, Johnson and Holubec, 1986) so students learn how to work effectively together. The small groups are perfect opportunities for students to learn about reaching agreements, listening attentively and how to encourage others on the team.

Inquiry learning

Yes, teachers can change the process by varying the modes of inquiry. Teachers use *problem-based learning, case studies, projects* and *performance tasks*. In each of these modes of inquiry, students are expected to take on the role of investigator. Students become responsible for 'uncovering' the content, rather than the teacher being responsible for 'covering' it. In each of these authentic learning models, students are at the centre of the learning.

Students become responsible for 'uncovering' the content, rather than the teacher being responsible for 'covering' it.

Problem-based learning is becoming a well-known model in which students 'meet' a real-world problem scenario and are expected to plot a path towards resolution. Along the way, of course, there are research tasks, interviews and investigations (Fogarty, 1997). The problem might address a social issue or a scientific concern. It often begins with the words 'You are ...' thus establishing the student's role as stakeholder as they address the problem area. Some teachers include the words 'You will …' as they delineate the requirements. ('You are a news reporter. You will discuss the media's role in the discussion of individual rights. How will you present your findings?') Differentiation is a given in these open-ended experiences.

Case studies (Fogarty, 1997) are often initiated with a vignette or story to introduce a moral or ethical dilemma. Students usually identify with a particular character and try to discern the key elements of the situation. A major component of the inquiry is in the ensuing debriefing discussion and the application of lessons to personally relevant situations. Differentiation is part and parcel of this model, because students relate personally to the cases. For example, the concept of addiction might be appropriately broached through the study of an addicted teen, delineating the recovery process.

Projects in science, humanities and the fine and practical arts involve research and investigations that are centred on the student (Berman, 1997). The project may result in a product or a performance, but it almost always involves real problem-solving and decision-making. These projects range in time from one class period to several weeks. Sometimes, the project requirements include a report of the findings as well. Students find their way through the project as differentiation is honoured. Illustrations of typical projects include service projects, historical projects and maths projects.

Performance learning focuses on the design and development of an authentic performance such as a musical production, a dramatic play, a gymnastic demonstration or practical demonstrations such as cooking or building. The performance becomes the instruction and the assessment all rolled into one. The 'proof is in the pudding', as they say. Performance learning often is accomplished by a performance rubric, delineating criteria and indicators of quality

What does it mean to differentiate instruction by changing the product?

To change with challenge and choice, three changes in product warrant discussion: *entry points* to learning, *expressive modes* of what has been learned and methods of *accountability*.

Entry points

To change the entry points to learning, Howard Gardner has provided a marvellous framework in his theory of multiple intelligences (1999). The eight intelligences include verbal–linguistic, visual–spatial, logical–mathematical, musical–rhythmic, bodily–kinesthetic, interpersonal, intrapersonal and naturalist. According to the theory, each of us has a jagged profile of these intelligences that is as unique as our fingerprints. By changing the entry points, students work through their strengths and thus differentiation will be there in the final product. If students choose to draw their perception of a story the product is predetermined.

By observing how children interact with the learning environment the teacher gathers clues to the various entry points of learning that work best for particular students. Armed with this information and an enriched learning environment of many choices, teachers can direct students toward accessible entry points to help them learn more easily (Fogarty & Stoehr, 1995).

In addition to the teacher's evaluation of entry points, students can become skilled at assessing their own strengths and weaknesses. When they know how they learn best, students can make informed choices about their own entry points to learning. Between the teacher's understanding and the student's awareness of the multiple intelligences approach, learning can be customised or tailored for optimal student achievement. For example, if a student is a visual learner a visual–spatial approach to learning mathematics information might work well. This student might create a graph and incorporate relevant details of their learning into tables and charts. In another scenario, the learner may be very logical–mathematical in their thinking and prefer to learn about the geographical region through a computer software program. Still another student, who seems to learn best in an interpersonal mode, may choose to work with a partner to display their understanding of the mathematical equations.

Students can make informed choices about their own entry points to learning.

The idea of different entry points doesn't mean that the teacher must offer eight learning options to every lesson or that all eight intelligences must be a part of every lesson. It simply means that learners need some options in how they go about their learning. Thus, when

■ □ ■ □ ■

teachers design the learning situations they need to plan for several possible entry points.

It is important to point out that most complex learning tasks integrate several intelligences into the overall picture. So, the student who is doing a hands-on approach could also be using an interpersonal or a musical–rhythmic approach along with the bodily–kinesthetic. Or, the logical–mathematical learner might use the intrapersonal as well as the visual–spatial as they work at the computer. And, in turn the visual–spatial learner could combine the bodily-kinesthetic with the naturalist as they represent their learning pictorially, using collage as their medium.

Expressive modes

Just as learners have propensities for entering learning through different doors, they also may exhibit preferences for expressing their learning in different ways. To change the exit points for expressing what one knows and is able to do, teachers can again use the theory of multiple intelligences as a framework. Let students choose the expressive mode or modes that work best for them.

They can express their understanding of the learning using Armstrong's 'smart' version of Gardner's work – word smart, logic smart, art smart, nature smart, self smart, people smart, music smart and body smart (Armstrong, 1999).

For example, if they are 'logic smart', let them express themselves electronically using all the skill they have with logical, deductive reasoning to navigate complex computer software. If students are 'art smart', let them depict their artistic thinking through one or more of the visual arts. If students are 'nature smart', let them tap into the areas of environmental learning and assessments. If they are 'people smart', let them lead the teams in learning investigations and explorations, and organising group presentations of their findings. If students are 'self smart', lead them towards introspective kinds of learning and evaluation tools. If they are 'music smart', encourage them to use the medium of music to express their understandings. If they are 'body smart', let them express their learning through dance, drama, mime or puppetry.

In short let students determine, as much as possible and whenever possible, how they might best demonstrate what they know about a particular topic and how they can apply that learning in relevant ways.

> **Let students determine, as much as possible and whenever possible, how they might best demonstrate what they know.**

Accountability

One other way to differentiate learning is to change the accountability factor. That is not to say that students are not responsible for the learning. It means that teachers provide different ways for students to be accountable for the learning. They vary the accountability measures whenever possible and look for a robust picture of that student learning. To change the method of keeping students accountable, use a balance of assessment methods (Fogarty, 1998) that include *traditional assessments, portfolio assessments* and *performance assessments.* In this way students have ample opportunity to depict the evidence of their learning.

Teachers differentiate traditional assessments by allowing an oral exam rather than a written exam; by frequently changing the kinds of quizzes they give; and by permitting students to re-take and re-test.

By incorporating the use of student portfolios teachers gain a different perspective about what students have learned. Portfolios provide real artifacts of learning that demonstrate growth and development. They enhance the information obtained from the tests. In fact, the portfolio is a true reflective tool that acts as a self-reflective method as well as providing visual evidence of learning. Portfolios might be simple work folders, more elaborate 'showcase portfolios', or even electronic portfolios, but in all models they contain artifacts of student work – writing, outlines, pictures, photos and reflections on all of these artifacts.

Portfolios provide real artifacts of learning that demonstrate growth and development.

Finally, the balance of different methods of accountability is completed with the addition of performance assessments. By requiring students to demonstrate what they know and are able to do, teachers have another dimension of student learning. The performance is the proof that students really understand and can apply the learning. It takes the learning from inert knowledge to concrete application. Performance includes, among other things, role-plays, drama, musicals, speeches, debates and presentations that are 'scored' with rubrics of criteria and indicators of quality.

In brief, when the teacher uses differentiated methods for holding students accountable student differences are honoured and a full picture of student accomplishments is the result. The combination of the three methods provides a rich portrait of student learning and seems to be a responsible approach to assessment.

How do teachers prepare for differentiating instruction?

According to Carol Ann Tomlinson, there are simple things teachers can do to differentiate instruction – lo-prep ideas – and there are more complicated things teachers can do – high-prep ideas.

Lo-prep

Teachers can use a variety of techniques that are lo-prep, but the message is, 'Begin slowly; just begin'. Among the lo-prep ideas are: offering homework options, choices among books, working together alone option, flexible seating, open-ended activities, varied modes of expression, explorations by interest, mini-workshops, negotiated criteria, goal setting, reading buddies and computer mentors.

> **Use a variety of techniques that are lo-prep, but the message is, 'Begin slowly; just begin'.**

Many of the lo-prep strategies – work together alone, computer mentors, reading buddies – involve cooperative learning. It's fairly easy for the teacher to give students the option of working with someone else because 'the power of two' is well documented in the literature. Cooperative learning partners can dialogue as they problem-solve and reflect on their learning. Lo-prep mini-lessons are formed of flexible skill groups that teachers use to revisit, re-teach and/or extend skills.

Negotiated criteria as a lo-prep strategy, means criteria that develop from conversations with the student or small group and the teacher. They decide together the criteria that will be used to judge the work. Student/teacher goal setting is similar to negotiated criteria, but goal setting is more long term. A student sets a goal to read so many books for the term, while the same student negotiates three criteria for the research project due next week.

High-prep

High-prep means the teacher needs time to plan the strategies and implementation usually occurs over time. Examples of high-prep strategies include: independent studies, learning contracts, literature circles, choice boards, simulations, problem-based learning, learning centres, interest groups, compacting curriculum and community mentoring.

> **High-prep means the teacher needs time to plan the strategies and implementation.**

Compacting learning is high-prep because the teacher must determine what the student already knows about a topic before they can allow the student to skip the mastered material and go on directly to new, challenging material. Teachers in essence compact the material and allow students to move forwards.

Problem-based learning is an inquiry-based approach to learning. Students are given an open-ended scenario or problem, a stakeholder role is identified and they are required to investigate and come up with some alternatives. An example scenario: The river is polluted and killing all the fish. You are the mayor of the town and citizens want something done about the situation. What will you do?

One of the primary ways to differentiate is to let students group themselves by interest. Many of the high-prep strategies – community mentorship, interest groups, choice boards – involve giving students many options to choose from. For example, within a classroom unit on DNA and the study of the human cell, students can form interest groups for the research portion of the unit – they can choose to research the particular genetic disease that interests them from a list of such diseases.

One of the primary ways to differentiate is to let students group themselves by interest.

Choice boards offer many options for students to select from as they study a particular unit – students may choose to study a famous person by reading a chosen biography, creating a puppet show, developing a *PowerPoint* presentation or by writing letters about the person. Mentoring is a long-term opportunity for students to learn from an expert – students might be mentored in maths, architectural design or journalism. However this depends on who is available to mentor.

'Literature circles' is a structured small group process for reading and studying a novel, short story or similar fictional genre. The circle has member roles, assigned chunks of reading and discussions that revolve around the various assignments of the members. For example, the 'literary luminary' reads favourite passages from the text; the 'discussion leader' leads the conversation with key questions; the 'vocabulary enricher' shares selected word definitions; and the 'illustrator' creates a descriptive cover illustration.

Teachers design independent studies with certain required criteria. This is often done with the cooperation of the student who may know more about the topic. However, the teacher has to ensure it fits with the standards of the curriculum.

How do differentiated classrooms compare to traditional classrooms?

According to Carol Ann Tomlinson, the major areas of difference between a differentiated classroom and a traditional classroom include: teacher roles, student roles, instruction, curriculum and assessment strategies.

In differentiated classrooms student interest is often used as a tool for differentiation.

In a differentiated classroom the teacher facilitates students' abilities at becoming self-reliant, while in the traditional classroom the teacher takes over control and directs student behavior. Traditionally, the teacher is the primary problem-solver in the classroom, yet in the differentiated classroom both the teachers and students solve problems.

In terms of the student role, a narrow sense of intelligence prevails in the more traditional classroom, while in the differentiated classrooms the focus is on multiple forms of intelligence and learning profiles. In traditional classrooms student interest is infrequently tapped, while in differentiated classrooms student interest is often used as a tool for differentiation.

Assessment in differentiated classrooms is ongoing and diagnostic.

Instruction in the differentiated classroom uses multiple materials, perspectives and multiple option assignments. There may be whole group introductions to material, yet individual and small group instruction dominates.

Assessment in differentiated classrooms is ongoing and diagnostic in order to make the instruction more responsive to learner needs. Excellence is largely defined by individual growth from a starting point.

Activity 1: Differentiating instruction inventory

After learning about the three ways teachers differentiate instruction, take an inventory of your own lesson plans and things you already do. Identify one example of each: changing the content, changing the process and changing the product

Activity 2: Compare and contrast

Create your own Venn diagram comparing and contrasting traditional instruction to differentiated instruction. Share your diagram with a colleague.

What do you think?

Review the following agree/disagree statements and respond to each. After you have finished, discuss your answers with a partner.

1. Differentiating instruction does not involve 'changing the standard'.

2. Changing the complexity means moving from the concrete to the abstract.

3. Changing resources in classroom instruction is a common practice.

4. Cooperative learning is a viable strategy to change the process.

5. The process model that almost automatically differentiates is problem-based learning.

6. The multiple intelligences approach to learning is practiced by some teachers.

7. The major kinds of assessments discussed for differentiation include performance assessments.

8. Lo-prep ideas for differentiation include compacting the curriculum.

9. High-prep ideas for differentiation include preparing case studies.

10. Differentiated classrooms value individual learning profiles.

Inside the classroom and beyond

While most teachers practice some differentiation, think about how you might begin to do more to differentiate instruction in your classroom. Discuss the idea with the students and get their input about how they learn best. Then, try to think of several lo-prep things you can do to get started.

Chapter 3: Identifying student needs

This chapter puts the focus on the students. It discusses the wide range of student needs and how teachers begin to address those needs across a continuum of skills. The chapter also presents information on how teachers identify student needs and the role of achievement data as a tool for informing instructional decisions for differentiating instruction. In addition, the concept of flexible skill grouping is examined as one of the most important and viable strategies for differentiating instruction.

The chapter addresses the following questions:

How do teachers address the different levels of readiness students exhibit?

What are the differentiation continuums and how do they help teachers differentiate instruction?

How do teachers identify individual student needs and apply the continuum of ideas?

How does student data relate to identifying needs and to differentiating instruction?

What is flexible grouping and how does it help in differentiating instruction?

How do teachers address the different levels of readiness students exhibit

Before teachers can become adept at addressing specific needs of individual students, teachers must begin with at least a foundational dichotomy in approaches. This dichotomy involves addressing the needs of the less developed students and, at the same time, addressing the needs of the more advanced students.

> **To address the range of readiness levels is to identify what students know and what they don't know.**

One of the first and foremost things teachers can do to address the range of readiness levels is to identify what students know and what they don't know. The teacher then must have the ability and the willingness to act upon that information. With the less developed students, teachers must identify and make up the gaps in their learning as quickly as possible. On the other hand, with advanced students teachers must allow them to skip the practice of mastered material and go forwards with their other challenges. It is so hard to help students make up and catch up with missing material, and it's equally hard to let students skip something even when teachers know the students know it.

For the varied readiness levels teachers find the use of more *direct instruction* methodologies with the struggling students seem to work best, while with the advanced students teachers tend to allow more *independent activities* and products. For example, teachers may lead a lesson on the use of adverbs in a direct instruction approach, while with more advanced students they require writing with evidence of three adverbial phrases.

Typically, teachers provide more *structured activities* with known parameters for the less developed learner, while they prefer very *open-ended activities* for the more advanced students. Structure, in terms of a class report, might mean the teacher schedules due dates for note cards, outlines, first drafts, final drafts and presentations, while open-ended might mean the teacher designs a class report with many options about content, focus and methods of presentation.

> **Teachers provide more *structured activities* with known parameters for the less developed learner ...**

Often, teachers design *simpler activities* for struggling learners, with more *complexity* added in for the more advanced learner. For example, a skilled teacher may require some students to use their spelling words in context by writing complete sentences for each word. On the other hand this teacher may require advanced learners to use the words in context, by using the words in a paragraph or, with even more complexity, by using the words in a three-paragraph essay. The skill is similar but the tasks range from simpler to more complex.

Teachers may use *concrete* activities by having some students actually utilise the six simple machines (pulley, wheel, wedge, inclined plane, screw, lever) in the construction of a working 'dragon', while other students may be asked to create verbal metaphors of six simple machines, using a more *abstract* format.

Using *fewer steps* to achieve a task is a strategy for less developed students while the more advanced students may be required to incorporate *multiple phases* to a project. An illustration of this involves the three-step process to writing an essay: Paragraph 1, beginning; Paragraph 2, middle; Paragraph 3, end. More advanced students may be asked to develop a persuasive essay supported by an electronic presentation of the key points with no steps actually outlined for them.

Teachers frequently use a deliberate pace when addressing less developed students, while with more advanced learners they allow the students to set their own pace. With a maths project on finding the area of their bedroom walls, the process may be paced quite deliberately: Step 1, measure the walls; Step 2, add the sums together; Step 3, decide to paint or paper and explain why; Step 4, figure out the amount of paint or paper needed. With advanced students the assignment is given holistically: Find out how much paint or paper you need to redecorate your bedroom.

What are Tomlinson's differentiation continuums and how do they help teachers differentiate instruction?

Teachers can differentiate information, materials and applications along a continuum from *foundational* to *transformational*. They can move from ideas that are close to the text to ideas quite removed from the experience; from fundamental skills to permutations of skills far beyond the fundamentals. At one end of the continuum students experience near or automatic transfer, while at the far end of the continuum they must seek more mindful applications that are somewhat remote from the initial learning situation. For example: foundational is doing skill drills in maths; transformational is applying the principles of maths to a real-world problem.

At one end of the continuum students experience near or automatic transfer, while at the far end of the continuum they must seek more mindful applications.

In the most basic of ways, teachers can differentiate instruction along the continuum from the *concrete* to the *abstract*. Hands-on

■ □ ■ □ ■

learning is concrete by nature, while 'book-learning' tends to be in the abstract.

By moving from the *simple* to the *complex* teachers can differentiate instruction along a broad-reaching continuum. Simple does not mean easy or watered-down, it means straightforward and clear. Complex means the task has layers and intricacies involved. Simple can be the crystal clear definition of the process of life cycles. Complexity can be added by requiring several examples of life cycles that depict its meaning.

Using a *single facet approach* as opposed to a *multiple facets approach* is one way for teachers to differentiate instruction. Simply put, by requiring few steps, fewer parts, fewer stages and phases, the task is made more accessible to developing learners. When preparing students to give a talk, simplified steps might include:
1. Opening; 2. Message; 3. Closing. However, in a multifaceted approach, the 'talk prep' might include:
1. Opening; 2. Quote; 3. Message; 4. Visual; 5. Review; 6. Closing.

When there are few unknowns, when there is relative comfort with most elements, when 'the leap is a small one, rather than a great leap', students are more likely to grasp an idea with ease and learning is evolutionary. At the furthest end of this continuum, when there are many unknowns and relative unfamiliarity requiring flexible thought, learning becomes more revolutionary for the advanced learner. Using the text outline to learn about the American Civil War is evolutionary, while studying the Gettysburg Address to extrapolate the meaning is revolutionary.

As mentioned earlier, teachers can move from very structured situations along a continuum to more open situations; more directions to fewer directions; more modelling to less modelling; little student choice to lots of student choice. When teachers use lab experiments they provide very specific scaffolding for safety procedures for less developed learners, while more advanced learners are shown once or twice and then given more independence to proceed.

Using a continuum from well-defined problems to fuzzy/ill-defined problems; from only providing relative data to providing extraneous data; from a specified problem to an ambiguous situation, teachers are able to differentiate instruction for many types of learners. A structured problem might involve cleaning litter from the playground as a recycling project. A fuzzy problem might involve the moral dilemma of how to deal effectively with bullies.

> **In the theory known as 'Vygotsky's zone of proximal development', the teacher gradually moves from a strong position of instructional guidance to a position in which the student is eventually working fairly independently.**

Again, moving along a continuum from heavy teacher involvement to less explicit teacher guidance – from student/teacher dependence to student/teacher interdependence, from much scaffolding to little scaffolding – the instruction can be differentiated to fit the needs of various learners. In brief, teachers guide the learning closely with struggling readers using guided reading strategies, while more advanced readers read independently with assignments done on their own.

In the theory known as 'Vygotsky's zone of proximal development', the teacher gradually moves from a strong

■ □ ■ □ ■

position of instructional guidance to a position in which the student is eventually working fairly independently. The gradual release of responsibility on the part of the teacher is intentionally orchestrated as the learner gradually becomes more competent at the task. Often this concept of gradual release of responsibility is referenced with reading skills and comprehension strategies, but it applies to all kinds of learning situations.

How do teachers identify individual student needs and apply the continuum of ideas?

Teachers need to consider physical, emotional, social, intellectual and academic needs, as well as the multiple intelligence profiles of student strategies and instruction.

Physical characteristics which affect student strategies and instruction include: size, stature, height, and weight; visual and auditory acuities; mobility or physical impairments of any sort; and general appearance, grooming and the demeanour of the student.

Teachers need to be aware of *emotional characteristics* that include: emotional stability, maturity and evidence/level of coping skills. In terms of *social characteristics*, teachers must consider the ability of the student: to get along with others, to fit in, to be comfortable alone or in a minority position on an issue; student preferences to lead or to follow, to be a team player, to argue or to mediate; to go along or to isolate.

Intellectual characteristics include: general intellectual abilities, specific aptitudes, intellectual curiosity; as well as opportunities for intellectual stimulation through family, friends and lifestyle, and through student interests.

Academic characteristics are defined separately from intellectual abilities. Academic attributes are about how the student performs in school tasks or uses their abilities. It's about the student's willingness to learn, their persistence at a task, pride in their work and ability to demonstrate a sense of accomplishment in a task well-done.

Using Gardner's eight intelligences it is often appropriate for teachers to survey the students to determine their strengths and weaknesses in the following 'intelligences': verbal–linguistic, visual–spatial, interpersonal–social, intrapersonal–introspective, musical–rhythmic, mathematical–logical, bodily–kinesthetic, and naturalist–physical world. Based on these assessments teachers can foster differentiation.

It's important to appraise students' family history. Does the student have siblings in the school? Who are the family members who live in the home? Who is the guardian contact? Does the student walk, ride, take a bus? Bring a lunch or buy it from the tuckshop? Is there a pending situation? Divorce? Adoption? Sick relative? The more the teacher knows about the student the easier it is to accommodate the needs of that student.

It's important to appraise students' family history.

It's important to appraise *students' interests* and areas in which the student excels and has intrinsic motivation. Often these are entry points to learning for the student. After all, we all like to do what we are interested in and what we are good at. In fact, sometimes these two are the same and it becomes an obvious tool for teachers to use to differentiate instruction. Both student interests and student ability are differentiating tools.

How does student data relate to identifying needs and to differentiating instruction?

In many cases the area demographics provide valuable information regarding the ratios of minority populations, English language learners (ELL), socio-economic levels, mobility rates, graduation stats, drop-out percentages and 'big picture' kinds of disaggregated data that feed into the specifics of school building demographics such as year level, classroom and student data. Data from the area level help teachers determine materials and supplies that are best suited to their particular populations.

On the other end of the spectrum is classroom data gleaned by teacher observations, anecdotal records, student work portfolios, marks, rankings and work habits. This kind of personal information, gathered over time, supports the teacher's view of the student and helps guide the methods and materials that seem appropriate.

Perhaps some of the most misunderstood yet valuable data to guide the differentiation of instructions come from the state test data that is more often than not aligned to the state standards of learning. This test data, when managed properly, can provide very specific student lists for flexible skill groupings.

Test data are often used as cumulative assessments about schools, classes and entire areas. The data are published in newspapers, used to formulate federal funding for the schools and even used by real estate agents marketing housing sales in the area. This use of the state assessment data looks at overall scores; comprehensive information about the number of students who 'do not meet', 'meet', or 'exceed' state standards.

Perhaps some of the most misunderstood yet valuable data to guide the differentiation of instructions come from the state test data.

The real value of the same data, used for instructional decision-making, can easily be overshadowed. Yet just looking at the number of students in the 'four quartiles' – the top 25%, the high-middle 25%, the low-middle 25% or lower 25% – can provide visible, accurate and accessible starting points for instructional interventions.

In addition to looking at general quartile scores, specific reading skills can be revealed with data management software programs. For example, a group of names is highlighted for the skill of making generalisations, based on the item analysis. In time, all schools will have immediate access to delineating sub-groups for skill work in reading, maths and all other disciplines tested.

Using a 'data ladder' to sort and define skill groups for instructional interventions doesn't mean these students will be tracked.

Using a 'data ladder' to sort and define skill groups for instructional interventions doesn't mean these students will be tracked in low, middle and high performing tracks. It means that specific attention will be given, temporarily, to certain 'steps on the ladder' for explicit and immediate instructional intervention strategies to improve that specific skill area. These groupings change often.

■ □ ■ □ ■

Generally, flexible skill groups are defined as temporary student groupings based on skill deficit areas. These skill groups change as improvement in the skill occurs. Frequent assessments or local assessments are used to provide data for these ever-changing skill groups. In tracking models, the group is designated and remains as the status quo throughout the year or even an entire school career.

Flexible skill groups are defined as temporary student groupings based on skill deficit areas.

What is flexible grouping and how does it help in differentiating instruction?

Usually, the size of the flexible skill groups are somewhat small, perhaps 5–8 students who indicate a need in a certain skill area. If the group is larger than that the skill probably needs re-teaching for most of the class and it will be revisited in the general teaching arena.

Flexible skill groups change as frequently as there are indicators of mastery of a skill. Students are placed in the groups based on data that indicates the need for more work on particular skills (drawing conclusions) or sets of skills (comprehension). They are moved out of the group when there is evidence that the student is able to handle the skill with competence.

Again, local assessments or teacher assessments provide the necessary feedback for students to move in and out of the skill groups. These are truly instructional intervention groups with specific purposes in mind. They are not labels for a lifetime. In fact, many times teachers use pre- and post-tests, in addition to periodic tests, to determine entries and exits from the skill groups.

Unlike tracking, there is no stigma attached to the flexible skill groups. When students are in the group they know they are there for a specific purpose and that they can advance out of the group with effort and work. Tracking is more permanent and can cause a heavy emotional burden. Teachers tend to rotate students in and out of the skill groups at least quarterly, when local assessment data is available. In many cases, the skill groups are very temporary, with students being moved as teachers notice improvements.

There is no stigma attached to the flexible skill groups.

The most difficult part of flexible skill grouping is in gathering data often enough to make instructional decisions along the way. That is why, in some schools, testing has become an issue. If teachers aren't using the data to form skill groups they may feel there is too much testing. Nonetheless, skill groupings are effective ways to improve achievement and increase test scores.

The most difficult part of the flexible skill grouping strategy is in gathering data often enough to make instructional decisions along the way.

■ □ ■ □ ■

Activity 1: Read and reflect on learners

Using the information suggested in this chapter on developing/advanced learners, identify two students in your class, or one of your classes, and do a profile on those students. Include characteristics in these categories: physical, social/emotional, intellectual, academic, multiple intelligences and student aptitudes and interests. Try identifying a student at each end of the spectrum of needs – developing to advanced.

Activity 2: A jagged profile

A culminating activity involves using a multiple intelligences inventory with the students to determine the strengths and weaknesses in each students 'jagged profile of intelligences'. These inventories are available online. Just 'Google' the words *multiple intelligences inventory*. Try one with your class or one of your classes.

What do you think?

Review the following agree/disagree statements and respond to each. After you have finished, discuss your answers with a partner.

1. Readiness to learn and student interests are tools for differentiating instruction.

2. Identifying individual student needs is a first step toward differentiation.

3. Advanced learners may need to skip known material.

4. Less developed learners benefit from concrete examples.

5. Instructional pacing is a differentiating tool.

6. An important identifying characteristic for differentiating instruction is the social/emotional needs of students.

7. One continuum of strategies for differentiation is 'structured problems to open-ended problems'.

8. The important use of student achievement data provides information for teachers to act upon.

9. A viable strategy for determining instructional interventions is using flexible skill grouping.

10. Flexible skill groups are determined by the data.

Inside the classroom and beyond

Based on the input from this chapter about identifying student needs, talk to other resource people in the building about specific students and their learning needs. Develop an attitude of cooperation in determining how to best differentiate instruction for those students.

Chapter 4: Focus on the lesson

This chapter highlights 'the lesson' in the instructional process as opposed to the curriculum or the assessments. The lesson is typically defined as the learning experience or episodic activity, often depicted as a one period activity. Yet lessons are sometimes longer in duration, possibly occurring over several days. In this section teachers explore what it means to differentiate the lesson by readiness, interest or learning profiles. In addition there are further examples of changing the content, the process or the product to differentiate a lesson.

This chapter addresses the following questions:

What are strategies for differentiating a lesson?

How do teachers differentiate a basic lesson by changing the content?

How do teachers differentiate a basic lesson by changing the process?

How do teachers differentiate a basic lesson by changing the product?

What are generic elements of a basic lesson design?

What are strategies for a differentiated lesson?

The lesson is the instructional unit, the learning experience, the episode or the activity teachers employ as they teach their content. There are three basic considerations for differentiating a lesson: student readiness, student interests and student learning profiles (Tomlinson, 2001).

The lesson is the instructional unit, the learning experience, the episode or the activity.

Using data-based decisions students are assigned to flexible skill groupings for specific interventions. An example using maths problem-solving skills is that developing students might receive additional *time* and *attention* to problem-solving strategies while advanced students might be placed in a group for *compacting* the maths problem-solving curriculum, allowing them to skip practice assignments and move forward to more complex problems.

To tap into student's interests as a way to differentiate teachers often design *freedom of choice with a structure.* For example, students select from a list of comparable resources about democratic values. Choices are structured: a novel, the textbook, a biography or a primary source material such as the American Declaration of Independence. Also, *tiered activities* (same skill, but varied levels of complexity and abstractness) might be used.

One of the easiest ways to differentiate a lesson using learning profiles is through the framework of the multiple intelligences.

One of the easiest ways to differentiate a lesson using learning profiles is through the framework of the multiple intelligences (MI). Particular formats that work with the MI approach and address student interests include: *learning stations* (four different activities at four stations); *learning centres* (maths centre, language centre); *learning contracts* (written agreement between the teacher and the student); *choice boards, portfolios* and *agendas* (particular list of tasks to be completed by each student).

Within a readiness skill group teachers can allow student *choices* about the kind of work they will do at a *centre of learning.* Teachers may use *flexible skill*

■ □ ■ □ ■

groupings based on student achievement data and, at the same time, encourage students to select their method or product. For example in a science unit on DNA students may need extra help in learning concepts, but they can choose an Internet search, research method or a hands-on lab activity that develops the concepts.

> **Teachers may use *flexible skill groupings* based on student achievement data.**

One example is in literature circles, *selecting one book* from a selection of five books that have a similar theme but different levels of difficulty and different approaches. This is a strategy that taps into student interests. Their *selection of the role* in the literature circle taps into their MI learning preferences or profile strengths ('vocabulary enricher'/verbal–linguistic, 'discussion leader'/interpersonal-social, 'literary luminary'/visual–spatial).

How do teachers differentiate a basic lesson by changing the content?

To revisit this idea of changing content means to change the complexity of the content, the resources in which the content is available and the environment or context in which the content is learned.

It's not necessarily a harder activity but one that *goes deeper into* and/or *more broadly across* a topic. Learning about economics can be a simple lesson on supply and demand or it can begin with supply and demand, and then move students to analysing the supply/demand graph of a stock on the exchange.

An example of *changing resources* as a way of differentiating content is to have students gather news through one of the following sources: *The Age, The Australian, Australian Financial Review, Sydney Morning Herald or ABC Online.*

All learning is *contextual*, so when the teacher changes the learning environment they are essentially changing the environment. For example, when students are developing an expository report about a recent medical breakthrough, they might do it in the comfort of the classroom with the teacher readily available for help; they might to go the computer lab so they can edit and revise easily with various software programs; or they may want to use the library for its accessible resources. Each provides a different context for the work.

> **For advanced learners the teacher simply 'tweaks' the lesson up and pushes the students into more sophisticated material and more abstract ideas.**

> **With the struggling learners, the teacher 'tweaks' the content down a notch.**

It's not that hard for teachers to change the content of a lesson. Teachers are resourceful people and students might also be encouraged to bring in various resources. To differentiate a basic lesson for advanced learners the teacher simply 'tweaks' the lesson up and pushes the students into more sophisticated material and more abstract ideas. Students may be asked to read, take a position and justify their thinking. With the struggling learners, the teacher 'tweaks' the content down a notch with simpler approaches to the information. Students may be asked to summarise the information. Revisiting this idea, to change the process of the lesson means to change the elements of the direct *instruction* models, using *cooperative structures* or *design inquiry models* of learning.

How do teachers differentiate a basic lesson by changing the process?

It's not really that difficult to vary the process, if teachers have robust instructional repertoires of student interaction strategies and if they are well-grounded in cooperative learning and inquiry models.

By varying the *emphasis on the various elements of the lesson* teachers can differentiate direct instruction. For example, for some learners the teacher will stress the motivational part of the lesson and put great creativity and energy into the 'anticipatory set' to hook the learners. For others they might stress the independent practice because of their higher ability levels.

One of the easiest ways to vary the cooperative learning structure is to *vary the size of the group*. Skillful teachers always use partners with students needing lots of active learning time. They may use a 'pair of pairs' for other students who have competent social skills.

To *change the inquiry modes* teachers can use problem-based learning (PBL), with its fuzzy problem and open-ended approach, or they can use a more structured investigation with known parameters and delineate the steps.

One of the easiest ways to vary the cooperative learning structure is to *vary the size of the group*.

To differentiate for advanced learners the primary focus is on the pacing of the learning. Let them soar, if they are ready to soar. The primary element to differentiate with developing learners is the amount and kind of

Let them soar, if they are ready to soar.

support and scaffolding provided for the learner. This guidance is absolutely necessary to help this learner succeed.

How do teachers differentiate a basic lesson by changing the product?

Revisiting another idea, to change the product means to *change the entry points*, the *end points* or the *accountability*. To *change the entry point* actually *changes the product* in many cases because the product is determined by what kinds of activities the student is doing. For example, if the student decides to enter the unit on poetry by listening to recordings of poetry and lyrics, the end product will most likely take a similar form.

To change the end point requires decisions on the part of the teacher and the student. Once they agree on an accepted product or performance the end point is set.

Teachers can change the accountability of the lesson by changing the assessment technique. They can use quizzes, portfolios, electronic portfolios or performance rubrics.

Changing the assessment is only difficult if teachers are rigid about marks and rankings. It takes more time and energy to mark a product or performance than to mark quizzes and more traditional measures of assessments.

Advanced learners need lots of ambiguity and open-endedness in their investigations and assignments. Challenge them! Let them become a little frustrated. Let them struggle a bit. And let them feel the exhilaration of accomplishing a difficult task. Let them celebrate their effort and take pride in their work.

For developing learners, one of the easiest ways to differentiate the product is by allowing for *clear choices* in terms of entry points for learning. Let students decide how they will begin their investigation or skill work. Let them work through their strengths. A learning standard is the goal of the learning. It can be a content standard (maths, science etc.) or a process standard (thinking, technology etc.).

What are generic elements of a basic level design?

The *hook* is the motivator of the lesson. It gets the students interested and intrigued. It's the taste, the sampling of what's to come. When you differentiate the hook it taps into the creative genius of the teacher. It might simply be a quote or a puzzle; it might be a guest speaker or a video clip; or it could be a role-play or even an excursion. The *input* of the lesson is *what the teacher does* to provide information for the learning.

The *input* could be a lecture or mini-lecture; it might be a problem or a scenario; or it could be a set of principles to apply or rules and guidelines for the activity. The *interaction* of the lesson is *what the students do* to learn the information and how they interact with the materials and with others to learn.

To differentiate the *interaction* in a lesson the teacher facilitates any number of cooperative tasks or investigations. They can orchestrate working alone, working together or working as a whole group.

The *product* of performance is the evidence of the learning. It may be a report, a diorama, a portfolio or a *PowerPoint* presentation; it could be a musical performance or a product from a software program. They differentiate the product by using lots of student choices and by incorporating the multiple intelligences approach to foster the role of the visual and performing arts in the final products or performances.

The assessment is the *accountability* piece in the lesson. It is how teachers know what the students know and are able to do, and how well students are able to do it. Assessments are differentiated by using a selection of traditional, portfolio or performance assessments. These will be discussed fully in Chapter 6.

Reflection in the lesson is the self-assessment piece. It's the moment to look back at what has occurred and assess its value and worth; its strengths and weaknesses. Reflective methods involve meta-cognitive questions that cause students to evaluate their work, their interactions and their learning.

Activity 1: The elements of a lesson

Compare this lesson template to the one you use.

HOOK: Motivational introduction …

INPUT: What the teacher provides …

INTERACTION: What the students do …

PRODUCT OR PERFORMANCE: Evidence of learning …

ASSESSMENT: Accountability piece

REFLECTION: Self-assessment

Activity 2: Preparing the lesson

Prepare a basic, typical kind of lesson using the template below. Teach the basic lesson.

HOOK: Motivational introduction …

INPUT: What the teacher provides …

INTERACTION: What the students do …

PRODUCT OR PERFORMANCE: Evidence of learning …

ASSESSMENT: Accountability piece

REFLECTION: Self-assessment

What do you think?

Review the following agree/disagree statements and respond to each. After you have finished, discuss your answers with a partner.

1. A lesson is the instructional unit of learning.

2. Differentiating a lesson involves student achievement data.

3. One consideration of differentiating a lesson is readiness.

4. Learning profiles examine the multiple intelligences.

5. Student interests are peripheral information.

6. Differentiating a lesson means changing the teacher.

7. To 'tweak' a lesson means to omit the lesson.

8. A traditional lesson calls for teacher input.

9. Pacing for advanced students is vital.

10. Lessons need to address a standard of learning.

Inside the classroom and beyond

Revisit the basic lesson and try some differentiating strategies. Try to incorporate student choice or learning profiles or flexible skill grouping: 'tweak it up' and 'tweak it down'; change the content; change the process; or change the product.

Chapter 5: Focus on curriculum

This chapter puts the focus squarely on the curriculum rather than on the instructional or assessment components. It addresses the role of state standards in shaping the curriculum and how differentiation can be part of that curriculum. In addition, twelve principles of the brain and learning are introduced to emphasise the role of brain-based choices within the curriculum to differentiate learning for students. Then four theoretical models provide broad frameworks for differentiating curriculum units and finally six curriculum models are discussed to facilitate the differentiation efforts.

This chapter addresses the following questions:

What are the elements for differentiating curriculum?

What are brain principles that guide differentiating curriculum?

What are the theoretical models for differentiating the curriculum?

What are student-centred curriculum models that differentiate learning?

What are the elements for differentiating curriculum?

There are two basic elements that come together in the differentiation of curriculum: one is the students and the other is the standards. Together they interact in many ways as teachers strive to differentiate learning. With the students teachers consider readiness, learning profiles and interests, while with the standards they consider content, process and performance standards.

Student readiness is a primary consideration as teachers look at the curriculum. The standards are the same for everybody but the readiness level for achieving the standard often determines how the student accomplishes the goal. One example of this is through curriculum mapping and curriculum alignment. Once teachers know how the science curriculum lays out for the year they are ready to find the gaps and overlaps in student achievement. Students who are deficient in certain areas can be targeted for interventions and students who excel in curriculum areas can be targeted for compacting the curriculum.

Learning profiles, such as learning styles and multiple intelligences, provide rich information for teachers as they incorporate as many opportunities as possible for student choice into the curriculum unit. When students have a choice they have more buy-in to the unit of activities. An example of this could be using an environmental studies unit in which students select their course of study – pollution, recycling etc. – and the presentation style of their investigation – electronic presentation, dramatic role-play, position paper etc.

> **When students have some choice in the unit they have more buy in to the unit of activities.**

Student interests provide a natural differentiating tool in the curriculum unit. The teacher provides a rich array of choices for students based on their own particular values about a subject. Of course it is again freedom with a structure of options. In the above scenario of the environmental studies unit students are given choices about the focus of their investigation – air, water land pollutants – based on their interests.

The standards of learning are consistent across the board; they are the standards by which every student is judged. There are content standards for each discipline and year level, process standards that thread across the disciplines and performance standards that provide the indicators of quality for student understanding. The differentiation comes into play as teachers develop curriculum units that have rich and robust options to meet the goals of the curriculum. By prioritising the content standards into essential standards for mastery and supplemental standards for development, teachers can begin to differentiate the curriculum for advanced and developing learners.

An example of differentiating content standards is in fifth year maths, when the teacher/team designates numeracy, operations, problem-solving and measurement as essential standards for mastery and at the same time designate probability and metrics as supplemental standards for development. Advanced students may do independent activities with probabilities and metric while developing students may just touch on these ideas.

By designing the unit of study with lots of interactive activity options, the teacher automatically sets the stage for differentiating the curriculum unit. An example of activitiy options is embodied in the multiple intelligences. By offering opportunities for students to use their bodily–kinesthetic intelligence to build a model, or to use their visual–spatial intelligence to draw a diagram of the same information teachers are changing the process of how students study the unit.

■ □ ■ □ ■

Performance standards provide viable options for students as they work through the unit. They can meet or exceed the standard based on their own interest, motivation and effort. The ultimate performance is the driving test; most pass, but some pass with flying colours, while others just barely squeak by. Another example of a performance standard is writing a reaction paper to an editorial. The criteria include a stated position, supporting evidence and a concluding statement. All students must meet the criteria but differentiation occurs through the quality of the work. Some will excel and provide much supporting evidence, while others will simply meet the criteria with a sparse piece of evidence. Differentiation is built into the standard through the criteria in the scoring rubric. Rubrics are discussed in more detail in Chapter 6.

The ultimate performance is the driving test.

What are brain principles that guide differentiating curriculum?

Renate and Geoffrey Caine's seminal work Making Connections: *Teaching and the Human Brain* (1991) delineates twelve principles of how the brain learns. These twelve principles provide compelling rationale for differentiation.

Principle 1: Challenge engages the brain; threat inhibits it

In creating standards-based curriculum units teachers can include tiered activities that challenge but don't threaten different levels of learners.

Principle 2: Emotions and cognition are linked

Emotional involvement gets the brain's attention. Once the learner is attentive, short-term memory kicks in. Memory is the only evidence of learning. When planning curriculum units teachers include a variety of activities that tap into the emotions. Differentiation is inherent, as some students are motivated by one thing and some by another.

Principle 3: Learning involves both focused and peripheral attention

As teachers develop units of study around the standards they design activities to purposefully target the goals of the curriculum. But teachers also differentiate the curriculum unknowingly as students take away different understandings. For example, all of the students may understand how to find the circumference of a circle yet some students incidentally learn how to work with a partner, how to draw a perfect circle, etc. In fact 70% of learning is peripheral, so teachers must value the entire process of developing the curriculum.

70% of learning is peripheral.

Principle 4: The brain learns through parts and wholes simultaneously

Interestingly, some students prefer to learn by starting with the big picture while others prefer to start with the parts, skills or pieces. For example, one student looks at the whole decade that they are studying while another wants to dig into one specific area such as the music of the era. Both students will end up studying the entire unit.

Principle 5: There are two types of memory systems – implicit and explicit

Knowing that there are two types of memory systems, teachers can ensure that the curriculum is brain-based as well as standards-based by incorporating explicit memory activities that require practice, repetition and rehearsal, and at the same time fostering implicit memory by building on authentic experiences. For example, some students may want to memorise the periodic table of elements, while others learn best from lab experiences, actually using the elements.

Principle 6: The brain is a parallel processor

Developing curriculum that taps into all four lobes of the brain's neo-cortex helps differentiate curriculum. The four lobes include the frontal (thinking), the occipital (vision), the temporal (auditory) and the parietal (integration of the senses). Curriculum units that use many of the senses develop areas of visual activity and auditory experience. Higher order thinking naturally differentiates by student strengths.

Principle 7: Learning involves the entire physiology

Simply by being aware of the role of nutrition, exercise and relaxation in learning, teachers can differentiate curriculum. For instance they can weave movement into some of the unit activities and reflection into others. They can advocate nutritious meals and adequate sleep.

Principle 8: Each brain is unique

Probably one of the most relevant ways to differentiate curriculum is through the application of this principle. Each brain is unique, based on genetic codes and background experiences; based on nature and on 'nurture'. Teachers can design curriculum units with broad appeal to a wide range of learning profiles, abilities and interests. They can include individual, small group and whole group activities; role-plays and simulations; music and the visual and performing arts; reading, writing, speaking and listening activities; and tap into the many kinds of minds represented in each classroom.

Principle 9: Learning is embedded in experience

Most teachers understand the value of giving students the real experience rather than a representation of the experience. Taking the students to the zoo will always have more of a powerful learning impact than simply reading about the zoo. When youngsters come to school lacking in experiences teachers must try to create the experiences in creative ways.

Principle 10: The search for meaning is innate

When teachers utilise investigations and inquiry models of curriculum, student curiosity, interests and readiness levels help determine the investigative path each learner takes. Puzzles, conundrums, moral dilemmas and real-world problems are appropriate curriculum tools.

Principle 11: The search for meaning occurs through patterning

Using themes, principles, rules, theorems, big ideas and concepts are all ways to help differentiate the curriculum. Students need that perspective/context in order to make sense of things and fit the new material into their existing individual schema. That is differentiation at its best.

Principle 12: Learning always involves unconscious and conscious processing

The idea that learning continues even after the formal lesson, throughout the unit of study and even into the next units, is a call for a more connected and coherent curriculum. Differentiation is infused into curriculum units when there is time for reflection and connection making. Again each student makes their own connections but, in the end, they all have an understanding of the information.

> **Differentiation is infused into curriculum units when there is time for reflection and connection making.**

What are the theoretical models for differentiating the curriculum?

Four models that seem appropriate for differentiating curriculum include: Bloom's taxonomy of cognitive skills, Gardner's theory of multiple intelligences, Sternberg's triarchic theory of intelligence and Oliver Wendell Holmes' three-storey intellect.

■ □ ■ □ ■

Bloom's taxonomy

Bloom's taxonomy includes six levels. From the bottom level to the top there are: remembering, understanding, applying, analysing, evaluating and creating. To use Bloom's taxonomy to differentiate curriculum by having smart students use the higher levels (applying, analysing, evaluating and creating), and struggling students remain at the lower levels (remembering, understanding), is NOT sound practice for differentiating curriculum. All students can and must think at higher levels.

> **To use Bloom's taxonomy to differentiate curriculum by having smart students use the higher levels and struggling students remain at the lower levels is NOT sound practice for differentiating curriculum.**

Now let's look more closely at how these various levels can help differentiate curriculum in beneficial ways for all students. Teachers can differentiate the curriculum at the *remembering level* simply by changing the complexity of the knowledge input. While both groups can work off the same knowledge base advanced learners can use sophisticated material, while developing learners can use more basic materials.

For differentiation at the *understanding level* some students can demonstrate their understanding of a front-page news article by telling about it orally, while others might write a summary or a critique. Still others may show their depth of understanding by writing a parody of the original piece. In order to differentiate the *applying* and use of their learning in the curriculum unit on immigration, one group might do an annotated visual display to demonstrate their applied knowledge of the immigration process and requirements while another group might write to their local Member of Parliament to invite discussion on a parliamentary bill about immigration policy.

■ □ ■ □ ■

To differentiate at the *analysing level* the curriculum unit might offer options to compare and contrast two electoral candidates, to do a data analysis of a student survey on the upcoming election or to classify the various perspectives on key issues. All tasks require analysis, but there are differentiated choices.

At the *evaluating* level a curriculum unit on poetry can be differentiated by the use of several thinking/evaluating tools: the literary critique; a point system judgment; or a student-designed scoring rubric.

An example of differentiating the curriculum at the *creating* level is when teachers design options for culminating activities to the Aboriginal Australian studies unit. Some groups will synthesise their learning by acting out a play about various tribes; another may write a story about conflicts; still another group may create a diorama of certain turning points studied in the unit.

Gardner's theory of multiple intelligences

Gardner has identified eight intelligences which he defines as ways humans create products and solve problems. The intelligences include: visual–spatial, verbal–linguistic, interpersonal–social, intrapersonal–introspective, musical–rhythmic, logical–mathematical, bodily–kinesthetic and naturalist.

High *verbal–linguistic* skills include: reading, writing, speaking and listening. The differentiation comes as students choose options among the verbal skills, honing in on their strengths and developing their weaker areas. One student may be a great public speaker while another prefers to write their ideas.

The *visual-spatial* intelligence can be tapped in a differentiated curriculum unit by building in many opportunities for visual input. This is easy, as the data suggest that fully 70% of all input to the brain is visual. A curriculum unit targeting the use of

The data suggests that fully 70% of all input to the brain is visual.

technology can include activities with various graphic arts software: *PowerPoint* for presentation formats; *Excel* for graphic displays of information; digital photographs for portfolios of work; and web design tools for creating a website.

To differentiate curriculum with the *intrapersonal-introspective* intelligence requires specific reflection tools for students to use throughout a unit. This might include such things as lab booklets, double entry journals (write and pass to a colleague or teacher who responds) or learning logs with lead-ins ('I wonder …', 'I'm confused about …', 'The most exciting …'). Other reflective tools include: partner dialogues, daily journals and portfolios of student work.

Of course any curriculum unit provides fertile ground for lots of *interpersonal–social* kinds of cooperative interactions from partners, to a 'pair of pairs' (Kagan, 1990), to the 'people search' (students seek out others to talk and articulate ideas), the 'human graph' (students become a graph) and small group work with roles and responsibilities. In a unit on living things groups may be formed using mammals and reptiles or plants and animals; or students might work in pairs for their research and in small groups for the presentation.

■ □ ■ □ ■

To differentiate curriculum with the *musical–rhythmic* intelligence, teachers often incorporate several kinds of options that tell about a unit of study such as dinosaurs, energy or 19th century literature. They can run the gamut from music appreciation (using music to set the tone or mood), to composition (a rap or lyrics), to performance.

Differentiating a curriculum with the *mathematical–logical* intelligence is quite natural and easy for teachers to do.

Differentiating a curriculum with the *mathematical–logical* intelligence is easy. Teachers simply include learning experiences that require deductive reasoning (general to specific – tell about magnets, then play with them), inductive reasoning (specific to general – play with magnets, come up with rules), logical sequence (three-paragraph paper – beginning, middle, end), Internet search and other technology-enhanced activities.

To differentiate curriculum with the *naturalist* intelligence seems hard in some instances. For example, it's easy to include a nature walk in the study of seasonal changes, but how to use the naturalist intelligence in a unit on metric measurement? Gardner specifies that the naturalist intelligence is about the knowledge of the flora and fauna, but the caveat he claims is that our naturalist intelligence is used when we classify and organise.

To differentiate a unit using the *bodily–kinesthetic* intelligence, the teacher designs the unit with lots of hands-on learning that includes large muscle movement and fine motor activities. For example, a history unit could include fine motor activities such as using a keyboard, drawing and model building. Large muscle activities could include excursions, dramatic plays and lab experiments.

■ □ ■ □ ■

Sternberg's triarchic theory of intelligence

Sternberg's triarchic theory of intelligence uses a factored model similar to Gardner's, yet there are only three intelligences: the critical, the creative and the practical.

This *critical intelligence* offers ample opportunities for differentiating curriculum because it targets the critical or analytical side of thinking. In a curriculum unit on reading informational text students might have options to analyse the ideas by comparing and contrasting, using classification strategies or by creating analogies and metaphors. All four are analytical measures, but they vary in sophistication levels.

To differentiate curriculum using the *creative intelligence* teachers include lots of options for originality, elaboration, fluency and flexibility in products and performances. For example, in a unit about Australia's involvement in World War II, students might choose their own method of displaying their understanding of the events of the war. They could do a map, a play, a song, a flag, a puppet show or any number of other authentic products or performances.

> **The *practical intelligence* is the most interesting intelligence to differentiate.**

The *practical intelligence* is the most interesting intelligence to differentiate. For example, a curriculum unit on Federation might include a simulation of the referendum, a recreation of the Australian flag or role-playing the inauguration ceremony.

■ □ ■ □ ■

Oliver Wendell Holmes' three-storey intellect

The three-storey intellect is a marvelous framework for differentiating curriculum. Similar to Bloom's taxonomy, it collapses the six levels into three. It is based on this poem, *'There are one story intellects, two story intellects and three story intellects with skylights. All fact collectors compare, reason, generalize, using the labor of fact collectors as well as their own. Three-story men idealize, imagine, predict – their best illumination comes from above the skylight.'* Teachers put this poem on the wall and use it as a differentiating guide.

To differentiate curriculum using the one-storey intellect, curriculum activities revolve around 'gathering' information in a number of ways: listing, naming, identifying, recognising, summarising, telling and re-telling. One example of differentiating with the one-storey intellect might be in a unit on weather in which students are expected to gather data about the local weather for one week. They can choose to gather the information in a log, using a calendar or simply by writing journal entries.

The two-storey intellect focuses on 'processing' and somehow making sense of the gathered information. In the same weather unit the second storey activities might include options to graph the information, to compare the week to the same week last year or to classify the weather each day by cloud formations, precipitation and sunlight.

In the three-storey intellect model, the third storey asks for application of the ideas gathered and processed in the first two storeys. This level of activity includes predicting, hypothesising, making inferences and generally going beyond the given information. Again, using the same weather unit the third storey activities would require students to forecast the next week's weather, extrapolate patterns from the data or to develop experiments on cloud formations and precipitation.

What are student-centred curriculum models that differentiate learning?

Student-centred curriculum models include PBL, case studies, projects, service learning and performance learning.

PBL (Problem Based Learning) differentiates curriculum by structuring a 'fuzzy' problem and allowing students to determine their paths of investigation based on interests and emerging facts. One PBL unit focused on the broad problem of river pollution. The students gathered information, identified what they thought was the heart of the problem and pursued their investigation in different ways. Some groups conducted interviews with the town council, others went to state and national agencies, while others still went to the media for their information. In addition, each group came to their own conclusions, presented their findings and alternatives and advocated a different position or solution.

Case studies are developed around a scenario that presents a moral dilemma. Differentiation is a natural part of this curriculum model because students relate their personal experiences and try to come to some logical, reasoned decisions. A case study around the concept of what constitutes a lie is one example. The scenario talks about someone who intentionally lies to avoid punishment;

someone who tells a 'little white lie' to spare a friend's feelings; and someone who lies by avoiding saying anything. Students discuss the three situations and come to moral/ethical decisions about each.

Project learning is such a natural differentiating tool that it almost needs no elaboration. As students select their project focus, methods and presentation, differentiation is there. In a history class students are given choices about developing a project around a particular decade or around a particular area. Their projects are open-ended with many options available.

Service learning is like project learning, except the service learning project centres around a civic cause or interest. A recycling project is an example of service learning projects. Students can choose various aspects of the project to focus on.

Themes are umbrella ideas (change, cycles, patterns, structure) that create a focus for curriculum, but within the theme many activities are afforded for differentiation. The theme 'Rites of passage' for middle year students provides a robust field for differentiation. Students can choose a rite of passage – first trip alone, first kiss, driving, shaving etc. – to develop as an example of growing up and becoming an adult.

Performances differentiate curriculum because the performance has quality criteria attached to it.

Performances differentiate curriculum because the performance has quality criteria attached to it and the differentiation is possible through individual options. *Performance learning* requires the student to demonstrate their learning through an authentic product or performance. The performance can be of low quality to high depending on the elements witnessed.

■ □ ■ □ ■

Activity 1: Curriculum models inventory

Take a quick inventory of the various curriculum models you already use: (PBL, case studies, projects, service learning, themes etc.) Name one you want to know more about.

Activity 2: Planning using multiple intelligences

Take an existing curriculum unit that is familiar to you and incorporate Gardner's theory of multiple intelligences into it, making sure there are activities that tap into every one of the eight intelligences. Then allow some student choice as you implement the unit.

What do you think?

Review the following agree/disagree statements and respond to each. After you have finished, discuss your answers with a partner.

1. The curriculum changes frequently.

2. Standards do not set the bar.

3. Principles of the brain, such as 'Each brain is unique', make the case for differentiation.

4. In Bloom's taxonomy the higher levels include: analysing, evaluating and creating.

5. The three-storey intellect presents a curriculum framework.

6. Problem-based learning usually has one right answer.

7. Thematic curriculum units are only for primary years.

8. Student-centred models include service learning projects.

9. Learners are considered for differentiation in curriculum models by a combination of learning profiles, readiness and interests.

10. Gardner's theory of multiple intelligences offers a valid and viable model for differentiating curriculum.

Inside the classroom and beyond

Ask students to assess their own strengths and weaknesses according to the eight multiple intelligences. Use an informal inventory or have them go online to find one. Just 'Google' *multiple intelligences inventory* and many options will appear. Then have them determine which one they want to work on in the next unit.

Chapter 6: Focus on assessment

This chapter focuses on how teachers differentiate assessments. Using the concept of a balanced assessment system teachers employ three different kinds of assessment tools including traditional assessments, portfolio assessments and performance assessments. Traditional assessments refer to tests of all sorts; portfolio assessments look at collections of student work; and performance assessments target the actual demonstration of what students know and are able to do. Each of the three methods is explored fully as ways to differentiate assessment for students in order to get a full picture of their progress.

This chapter addresses the following questions:

What are the elements for differentiating assessments?

How do teachers differentiate with traditional assessments?

How do teachers differentiate with portfolio assessments?

How do teachers differentiate with performance assessments?

What else can teachers do to differentiate assessments?

What are the elements for differentiating assessments?

The three considerations are the same three student-centred considerations that have threaded through this entire course: student readiness, learning profiles and

Balanced assessments mean that teachers have an assessment plan that includes divergent methods of appraising student progress.

student interests. While the assessments must reflect what students know and are able to do, the concept of balancing assessments for differentiation is a common one. As suggested, balanced assessments mean that teachers have an assessment plan that includes divergent methods of appraising student progress. The three frameworks include traditional assessments, portfolio assessments and performance assessments.

Traditional assessments

Traditional assessments are quizzes, teacher-made tests, criterion referenced tests, chapter tests, norm referenced, and standardised tests; work samples, worksheets, and even homework assignments that are marked. Traditional assessments provide marks and rankings for the demographic data of a student and their standing in the state, area, school or class. A quick example of differentiating traditional assessments is illustrated when the teacher allows a youngster to respond orally to a teacher-made test regarding a unit of study. While the student is required to take the test, the teacher differentiates to get a better picture of what the student knows by eliminating the written part of the test.

Traditional assessments provide marks and rankings.

Portfolio assessments

Portfolio assessment is an appraisal tool that engages students in the systematic collection, selection and reflection of their work over a period of time. These portfolios range from work folders to showcase portfolios.

Portfolio assessments provide a visible record of growth and development, evidenced by artifacts of the student's work. The focus with portfolios is on self-assessments. They complement traditional assessment measures. Often teachers use student portfolios for the duration of a particular unit of study. They might use the portfolio as a 'multiple intelligences portfolio', requiring evidence of each of the eight intelligences used during the unit of study. Differentiation is built into this type of assessment because the portfolio approach is so personal.

Portfolio assessments provide a visible record of growth and development.

Performance assessments

Performance assessment is an authentic task that demonstrates not only what a student knows but also what they are able to do. It's the real thing rather than merely inert knowledge. A typical example of a performance assessment is the production of a persuasive essay that has specific criteria that might include: a clear position arguments to support the position, and a strong closing statement. Performance assessment, when supported by criteria, still allows for differentiation through the quality indicators. Students can meet and/or exceed the standard set.

Performance assessment is an authentic task that demonstrates not only what a student knows but also what they are able to do.

One type of assessment is not better than another. It's the combination of the different types that create balance in the assessment picture. As teachers develop their assessment plan they use the various types of assessments quite purposefully. In their skilful use of the balance of assessments, teachers automatically differentiate assessments.

■ ▢ ■ ▢ ■

How do teachers differentiate with traditional assessments?

Teachers can differentiate assessments using tests in a number of different ways. They can use surprise tests as an accountability factor during the unit of study; they can allow students to choose a test as a learning tool, providing extrinsic motivation to learn; and they can use tests as a way for students to raise their mark in a particular class.

When teachers design the tests, they can accommodate different learning profiles by incorporating various types of test questions.

When teachers design the tests, they can accommodate different learning profiles by incorporating various types of test questions. They can use a variety that includes some short answer questions with some student-constructed responses, such as short essay questions. Some students respond better to the short answer while others can show their learning best in an essay.

As discussed earlier, in order to differentiate with criterion-referenced tests that align to the state standards, teachers can take advantage of the de-segregation of skills to form flexible skill groups for appropriate interventions. For example, a sub group of students may emerge that needs work in comprehension skills in reading.

Using the traditional tests in the textbook that appear at the end of the chapter, the teacher has the option to assign different questions to different students or to differentiate assessments for different groups of students. In another way, the teacher can differentiate the chapter tests by allowing more time or allowing students to work together or alone.

To differentiate state level, norm-referenced tests, teachers have no control over the testing itself as the test is normed by following the same guidelines. But teachers can differentiate instruction based on the results. While IQ tests are no longer given across the board to entire classrooms of students, when IQ information is available the assessment can inform the instructional decisions. However teachers must be careful not to label students based on one test score, or at one point in time. This is exactly why the balance of assessments is preferred practice.

The traditional achievement test usually yields some data on sub-skill groups that teachers can use to form flexible instructional groupings for specific interventions.

The achievement tests are quite informative when used in this way, rather than using them as summative data.

To differentiate using aptitude tests is actually the purpose of this kind of test. It displays the specific aptitudes of a particular student which can inform student decisions about course options and program choices.

How do teachers differentiate with portfolio assessments?

Working portfolios are just that, a work in progress. This is the portfolio or folder of work that students use over time, collecting and selecting work for the final portfolio. It's easy to differentiate working portfolios because of the student selection process in which there are lots

> **Working portfolios are just that, a work in progress.**

of opportunities for student choices of what goes in and what stays in the portfolio.

The showcase portfolio is the one that is used in the final analysis. It is more finished, with a table of contents, learning goals, written reflections and an attractive container of some sort that has been developed by the student. Teachers differentiate with showcase portfolios simply by the nature of the portfolio itself, which is the sole creation of each student. These are frequently shared with partners, the teacher and with parents.

Electronic portfolios are just beginning to hit the classroom scene but the potential for these classroom or personal web pages is astonishing. The power of the electronic portfolio is its flexibility to change things, adapt to a different focus and to continually add the newest and richest pieces to the web page. Differentiation is inherent in the electronic portfolio and that's one reason they will soon flourish as a means of differentiating classroom assessments.

The power of the electronic portfolio is its flexibility.

The collection phase of the portfolio process can be differentiated simply by allowing student choice for some of the items. For example the teacher might require eight items based on the eight multiple intelligences and the students can add three others. The selection process is really where the differentiation shines most brightly because it is at this phase of the portfolio process that students look over all of the items in their working portfolio and select the items they want. Now, some items are a given as the teacher has already made some requirements, but there is still lots of room for individual choices.

The reflection stage is truly a platform for differentiation because this is where the students write reflections about why they selected a particular piece. They may have selected it because it shows growth, it's a work in progress, shows various stages and phases of a piece of work or because it's an example of a best piece of work.

The portfolio conference is optional, but in reality a portfolio implies that it is to be shown to someone, that it will have an audience. When conferencing is part of the portfolio process teachers often have practice sessions with peer partners to prepare students for the parent conference.

> **The reflection stage is truly a platform for differentiation because this is where the students write reflections about why they selected a particular piece.**

How do teachers differentiate with performance assessment?

Performance assessments are embodied in performance tasks, authentic products or real performances that demonstrate what students are able to do. Differentiation occurs in the process of using the scoring rubric to determine the quality of the work. The scoring rubric has four critical parts: the standard, the criteria, the indicators of quality and the points assigned for scoring.

The standard of learning actually provides the language for the criteria in the rubric. For example, if the English standard states that 'all students will show evidence of the proper use of grammar, spelling and punctuation in their

> **The scoring rubric has four critical parts: the standard, the criteria, the indicators of quality and the points assigned for scoring.**

written work' (Burke, 2004), the rubric should contain that same language.

Using the above example of an English standard, the *criteria* for the rubric on an expository essay would include the following: grammar, spelling and punctuation. Now these may be subsumed under the criterion of 'writing mechanics', as one criterion (leaving room for other criteria such as content or logic) but the criteria are the guideposts by which the essay is judged so they must link back to the standard. The differentiation comes into play when the indicators of quality are added.

The *indicators of quality* can range from a low end of 'does not meet' to 'meets' to the far end 'exceeds'. However, to ensure a more accurate scoring rubric the experts suggest using an even number of indicators, rather than odd. With three or five, it's easy to just use that middle line. When using four or six, the teacher looks more closely to decide more exactly, or to differentiate more clearly, about the quality of the work.

Four indicators of quality may be: developing, competent, proficient and distinguished. Notice how it is easy for teachers to judge the developing learner and the advanced learner when using four indicators of quality. A less formal structure might read: not there yet, moving in the right direction, right on target and bull's eye!

Four indicators of quality may be: developing, competent, proficient and distinguished.

Once the rubric is complete, with criteria and indicators listed, the teacher must describe each indicator more specifically as they provide the guidelines for quality work. This often appears as a table or matrix of sorts.

■ □ ■ □ ■

Let's look at the rubric for the expository writing example.
(Criteria are bold; indicators are with italics)

Rubric: Expository writing assignment on using animals for testing purposes

	Developing	*Competent*	*Proficient*	*Distinguished*
Mechanics (Grammar, spelling punctuation)	Much evidence of errors in grammar, spelling and punctuation.	Some evidence of errors in grammar, spelling and punctuation.	Little evidence of errors in grammar, spelling and punctuation.	No evidence of errors in grammar, spelling and punctuation.
Content (Clear, concise, complete)	Message not clear; rambling; no conclusion.	Message emerging; somewhat concise; evidence of a conclusion.	Message clear, concise; summary; conclusion strong.	Message crystal clear; synthesis, concise; convincing conclusion.
Logic (Sequence, opening, message, conclusion)	No clear beginning, middle or end.	Evidence of a beginning, middle and end.	Clear beginning, middle and end.	Strong beginning, middle and end.

Once the rubric is developed teachers share the rubric *before* the students begin the assignment. In that way there are no surprises as students are informed ahead of time how their work will be judged. In fact, as students become more familiar with rubrics teachers

Teachers share the rubric *before* the students begin the assignment.

often involve them in the process of developing the rubric. Differentiation is part and parcel of the rubric through the quality indicators. Some will do the essay with a passing mark, while others will excel.

The teacher can assign *points* to the various criteria and then add up the total. For example, each of the four indicators are awarded appropriate points that apply to each of the three criterion: 4 points for distinguished, 3 points for proficient, 2 points for competent and 1 point for developing. The judgments are made, points are added across and totalled, and differentiation automatically occurs.

Teachers can give more 'weight' to one criterion by developing what is called a 'weighted rubric'.

Teachers can give more 'weight' to one criterion by developing what is called a 'weighted rubric'. In this way, in the same example, the teacher can place more value on content than on mechanics at the higher years, and vice versa with the younger students who are just learning about the mechanics.

The checklist is the first draft of the criteria required.

According to Burke (2004), one way for teachers to move toward rubrics and weighted rubrics as part of their assessment plan is to begin with a check list. The check list is the first draft of the required criteria. Teachers and students can make the check list together and students will know what is going to be 'checked off' when they turn in their work. Eventually, the teacher can use the check list to develop a scoring rubric with indicators of quality and assigned points.

■ □ ■ □ ■

What else do teachers do to differentiate the assessment process?

Other ways teachers can differentiate assessment is by offering options to students to do an oral exam rather than a written exam; or to allow someone to read the exam to students who may have language deficits.

Another differentiation strategy is to pace the test for certain students and give it to them in manageable parts or several sections at different times. The student is responsible for the entire test but it is broken into bite size pieces. In addition, self-assessments are options that help differentiate the assessment process. Self-assessments can be used in conjunction with other assessments or separately. Interestingly enough, when self-assessments are used students are often harder on themselves than the teacher or peers would be.

Another differentiation strategy is to pace the test for certain students.

In a final look at differentiating assessments teachers can allow students to select their assessment technique. For example, in a problem-solving unit in maths, students could take the prepared test, develop a portfolio of their problem-solving strategies or demonstrate the learning through an authentic problem-solving performance.

Activity 1: Assessing your assessment approach

Take a moment to inventory your assessment plan to see if you have a balanced assessment approach. List the *traditional measures* you use; how and when you use *student portfolios*; and when you use *performances and products* as evidence of learning. Think about why you use various kinds of assessments at different times. Then think about how you differentiate assessments for students.

Activity 2: Developing a rubric

Use this opportunity to develop a scoring rubric for an essential content standard that you address.

1. Begin with the standard in mind.

2. Start with the check list.

3. Select criteria from the check list.

4. Add indicators of quality.

5. Develop descriptors for each criterion/indicator.

6. Assign points to each indicator level.

What do you think?

Review the following agree/disagree statements and respond to each. After you have finished, discuss your answers with a partner.

1. Balanced assessments mean the teacher helps students balance their marks.

2. Traditional assessments provide the most accurate information.

3. Growth and development are best assessed with student portfolios.

4. Performance assessment is valued because it shows what a student is able to do.

5. Teachers differentiate assessment by balancing various kinds of assessments in an assessment plan.

6. A scoring rubric includes standards, criteria and indicators.

7. Differentiating assessments requires knowledge and skill on the part of the teacher.

8. Ways teachers differentiate assessment include changing the pace of the testing.

9. Teachers need to _____in order to differentiate assessments and develop rubrics with the students.

10. Differentiating assessments requires planning.

Inside the classroom and beyond

Share the rubric with the students and apply it to an assignment. Discuss the results with the students. Talk about developing a rubric together and get their feedback.

Resources

Armstrong, T. (1999). *Seven kinds of smart: Identifying and developing your multiple intelligences.* New York: Penguin Putnam.

Bellanca, J. (1990). *Cooperative think tank I.* Melbourne, Australia: Hawker Brownlow Education.

Bellanca, J. (1993). *Cooperative think tank II.* Melbourne, Australia: Hawker Brownlow Education.

Bellanca, J. (1997). *Active learning handbook for the multiple intelligences classroom.* Thousand Oaks, CA: Corwin.

Bellanca, J. & Fogarty, R. (2004). *Blueprints for thinking in the cooperative classroom.* 2nd Edition. Thousand Oaks, CA: Corwin.

Berman, S. (1997). *Project learning.* Thousand Oaks, CA: Corwin.

Berman, S. (1999). *Service learning.* Thousand Oaks, CA: Corwin.

Bloom, B. S., Englehart, M. D., Furst, E. J., Hill, W. H. & Krathwohl, D. R. (1956). *Taxonomy of educational objectives: Cognitive domain, handbook I.* New York: David McKay Co.

Burke, K. (1999). *The mindful school: How to assess authentic learning.* Melbourne, Australia: Hawker Brownlow Education.

Burke, K., Fogarty, R. & Belgrade, S. (1994). *The mindful school: The portfolio connection.* Melbourne, Australia: Hawker Brownlow Education.

Caine, R. N. & Caine, G. (1991). *Making connections: Teaching and the human brain.* Menlo Park, CA: Addison-Wesley.

Chapman, C. (1993). *If the shoe fits: Developing multiple intelligences.* Thousand Oaks, CA: Corwin.

■ □ ■ □ ■

Chapman, C. & King, R. (2003). *Differentiated instructional strategies for reading in the content areas.* Thousand Oaks, CA: Corwin.

Chapman, C. & King, R. (2003). *Differentiated instructional strategies for writing in the content areas.* Thousand Oaks, CA: Corwin.

Costa, A. (1991). *School as a home for the mind.* Thousand Oaks, CA: Corwin.

Csikszentmihalyi, M. (1990). *FLOW: The psychology of optimal experience.* New York: Harper and Row.

Diamond, M. & Hobson, J. (1998). *Magic trees of the mind: How to nurture your child's intellignece, creativity, and healthy emotions from birth to adolescence.* New York: Dutton Books.

Fogarty, R. (1998). *Balanced assessments.* Thousand Oaks, CA: Corwin.

Fogarty, R. (1997). *Brain compatible classroom.* Thousand Oaks, CA: Corwin.

Fogarty, R. (1990). *Designs for cooperative interactions.* Thousand Oaks, CA: Corwin.

Fogarty, R. (2001) *Differentiated learning: Different strokes for different folks.* Melbourne, Australia: Hawker Brownlow Education.

Fogarty, R. (2001). *Finding the time and the money for professional development.* Melbourne, Australia: Hawker Brownlow Education.

Fogarty, R. (2001) *Literacy matters: Strategies all teachers can use.* Thousand Oaks, CA: Corwin.

Fogarty, R. (1997). *Problem based learning and other curriculum models for the multiple intelligences classroom.* Thousand Oaks, CA: Corwin.

Fogarty, R. (2001). *Making sense of the research on the brain and learning.* Melbourne, Australia: Hawker Brownlow Education.

Fogarty , R. (1991). *The mindful school: How to integrate the curricula.* Melbourne, Australia: Hawker Brownlow Education.

Fogarty, R. (2001). *A model for mentoring our teachers: Centres of pedagogy.* Melbourne, Australia: Hawker Brownlow Education.

Fogarty, R. (2000). *Ten things new teachers need to succeed.* Thousand Oaks, CA: Corwin.

Fogarty, R. (2001). *Student learning standards: A blessing in disguise.* Melbourne, Australia: Hawker Brownlow Education.

Fogarty, R. (2001). *Teachers make the difference.* Melbourne, Australia: Hawker Brownlow Education.

Fogarty, R. (2001). *Brain compatible classroom. 2nd Edition.* Thousand Oaks, CA: Corwin.

Fogarty R., & Bellanca, J. (1995). *Multiple intelligences: A collection.* Thousand Oaks, CA: Corwin.

Fogarty, R. & Pete, B. (2004) *The adult learner: Some things we know.* Thousand Oaks, CA: Corwin.

Fogarty, R. & Pete, B. (2005) *Differentiated learning: An anthology to reach and teach all students.* Melbourne, Australia: Hawker Brownlow Education.

Fogarty, R. & Pete, B. (2004) *Teaching and learning: An anthology for professional teachers.* Melbourne, Australia: Hawker Brownlow Education.

Fogarty, R. & Stoehr, J. (1995). *Integrating the curricula with multiple intelligences.* Thousand Oaks, CA: Corwin.

Fullan, M. & Stiegelbauer, S. (1999). *The new meaning of educational change.* New York: Teachers College Press.

■ □ ■ □ ■

Gardner, H. (1999). *Intelligence reframed: Multiple intelligences for the 21st century*. New York: Basic Books.

Gregory, G. & Chapman, C. (2002) *Differentiating instruction: one size doesn't fit all*. Thousand Oaks, CA: Corwin.

Gregory, G & Kuzmich, L. (2004). *Data driven differentiation in standards-based classrooms*. Thousand Oaks, CA: Corwin.

Holmes. O. W. (1914) *The poet at the breakfast table*. New York: Houghtin Mifflin.

Hunter, M. (1970). *Transfer*. El Segundo, CA:TIP

Jensen, E. (1998). *Teaching with the brain in mind*. Alexandria, VA: Association for Supervision and Curriculum Development. Printed in Australia by Hawker Brownlow Education.

Johnson, D., Johnson, R. & Holubec, E. (1986). *Circles of learning: Cooperation in the classroom*. Alexandria, VA: Association for Supervision and Curriculum Development

Kagan, S. (1990). *Cooperatrive learning resources for teachers*. San Juan Capistrano, CA: Resources for Teachers.

Lazear, D. (1998). *Eight kinds of smart*. Melbourne, Australia: Hawker Brownlow Education.

Lyman, F. & McTighe, J. (1998). Cueing thinking in the classroom: The promise of theory-embedded tools. *Educational Leadership, 45*(7), 18–24.

Moye, V. H. (1998). *Problem based learning in Social Studies: Cues to culture and change*. Melbourne, Australia: Hawker Brownlow Education.

Pete, B & Fogarty, R. (2005) *Close the achievement gap: Simple strategies that work*. Thousand Oaks, CA: Corwin.

Pete, B & Fogarty, R. (2004) *Nine best practises that make the difference*. Thousand Oaks, CA: Corwin.

Pete, B & Fogarty, R. (2004) *Twelve brain principles that make the difference*. Thousand Oaks, CA: Corwin.

■ ☐ ■ ☐ ■

Pete, B. & Duncan, C. (2004). *Data! Dialogue! Decisions! The data difference.* Thousand Oaks, CA: Corwin.

Sousa, D. (1995). *How the brain learns.* Reston, VA: National Association of Secondary School Principals.

Sternberg, R. (1988) *Beyond IQ: A triachic theory of human intelligence.* New York: Viking.

Sylwester, R.(1995). *A celebration of neurons: An educator's guide to the human brain.* Alexandria, VA: Association for Supervision and Curriculum Development.

Tomlinson, C. A. (1999). *The differentiated classroom: Responding to the needs of all learners.* Alexandria, VA: Association for Supervision and Curriculum Development. Printed in Australia by Hawker Brownlow Education.

Tomlinson, C. A. (1999, September). *Mapping a route toward differentiated curriculum.* Educational Leadership, *57*(1), 12–16.

Tomlinson, C. A. (2000, September). *Reconcilable differences: Standards-based teaching and differentiation.* Alexandria, VA: Association for Supervision and Curriculum Development, 6–11.

Tomlinson, C. A. & Kalbfleisch, L. (1998, November). *Teach Me, Teach My Brain.* Educational Leadership. Alexandria, VA: Association for Supervision and Curriculum Development, 52–55.

Tomlinson, C. A. (2003, October). *Deciding to teach all students.* Educational Leadership. Alexandria, VA; Association for Supervision and Curriculum Development, 6–11.

Tomlinson, C.A. (2001). *How to differentiate instruction in mixed ability classrooms.* 2nd Edition. Educational Leadership. Alexandria, VA: Association for Supervision and Curriculum Development. Printed in Australia by Hawker Brownlow Education.

Williams, R.B. (2001) *Cooperative Learning: A standard for high achievement.* Thousand Oaks, CA: Corwin.

Williams, R.B (2002.) *Higher order thinking skills: Challenging all students to achieve.* Thousand Oaks, CA: Corwin.

Williams, R.B. (2002). *Multiple intelligences for Differentiating learning.* Thousand Oaks, CA: Corwin.

CORWIN

A SAGE Company

The Corwin logo—a raven striding across an open book—represents the union of courage and learning. Corwin is committed to improving education for all learners by publishing books and other professional development resources for those serving the field of PreK–12 education. By providing practical, hands-on materials, Corwin continues to carry out the promise of its motto: **"Helping Educators Do Their Work Better."**